In God's Word

Devotional Studies for Women

NANCIE CARMICHAEL

HARVEST HOUSE PUBLISHERS, INC.
Eugene, Oregon 97402

IN GOD'S WORD

Photo Credit: Author photo © 1989 by Tim B. Gilman/*Virtue*

Copyright © 1989 by Harvest House Publishers, Inc.
Eugene, Oregon 97402

Library of Congress Cataloging-in-Publication Data

Carmichael, Nancie.
    In God's word : a book of life for daily living / Nancie Carmichael.
      p.   cm.
    ISBN 0-89081-705-7
    1. Meditations. I. Title.
    BV4832.2.C273   1989
    242—dc19   88-31787
                                                          CIP

Printed in the United States of America.

For Mother, who taught me
to love God's Word

CONTENTS

V: Developing Inner Beauty

VI: Fruit: Evidence of
a Relationship

PREFACE

My earliest childhood memories are of my mother. Upon awakening in the mornings, I would go look for her. Most often I found her in the kitchen at the table, coffee cup in hand, poring over the Bible. Mother—a farmer's wife, mother of seven, and leader in the community, got answers from that Book.

She never told me so directly, but I understood it years later as a young mother myself with small children. Our church had a morning Bible study that I enjoyed attending. But there were many Bible-study mornings when I packed up the kids and threw a diaper bag over my shoulder, only to discover that one of the children had a fever or an upset stomach. Then there were the times that I *did* get to the church only to find that the babysitter *didn't*, and what was the point of staying in the nursery?

It was after one such morning that I drove home from the church with tears of frustration. I believed God was interested in His children, but was He really interested in *me*? Me, with little ones and all that went with having small children—things like allergies, ear infections, and a never-ending stream of laundry? Did He care about my secret longings and dreams? Where did I fit into His grand scheme? It occurred to me as I took my Bible out of the diaper bag that there was nothing stopping me from reading it on my own. Here I was, a minister's wife, and I had never established a personal Bible study! I started digging in, and that was the beginning of a growing love and profound respect for the Bible.

God did speak to me through His Word. He showed me how to love my children, my husband and my neighbors. He encouraged me to pursue personal growth, to lay aside fears, to trust Him more. Later, when my husband was a senior pastor of a church, I taught a women's Bible study. Simply to place God's Word "on the table" and then see the results as women responded to what God was saying to them *personally* became one of the greatest joys of my life. (And yes, we arranged to have child care for young mothers!)

Then there was a period of time in my life when I felt that everything around me was eroding. My much-loved father died. My mother developed cancer. We moved away from an extended family and intimate friends and our large, progressive church. A close friend and I had a time of estrangement. I sent my first of five children off to college, with more soon to follow. All this happened within a few short years. It seemed I was standing on shifting sands, and they were running out to sea. My very predictable world was dissolving. My immediate reaction was to latch onto my husband, hoping he would not be going anywhere. He wasn't, but he wasn't interested in having a clinging wife, either. A secret panic and anxiety gnawed at me. Again, God's Word penetrated my confusion with truth: *Only in Him do we find ultimate security.* "Who shall separate us from the love of Christ? . . . For I am persuaded that . . . [nothing] shall be able to separate us from the love of God which is in Christ Jesus our Lord" (Romans 8:35,38-39). Through His Word He spoke to me: Take your hands off people and things. Seek God—let Him work. Revel in His strength and provision.

My life took on new peace and direction and I thought: *Finally! Now I can really fly!* The children were all in school and becoming more independent. I took on some new challenges such as work with the prison, a position on the local school board and writing projects. I loved the stimulation of doing new things and of making a difference in my community. But I began having some physical problems: chronic aching joints . . . fatigue . . . chest pains. After a frustrating year of lab tests and doctor consultations, the diagnosis was confirmed—Systemic Lupus Erythematosus, an autoimmune disease that attacks the joints and can also attack the major organs. It's a chronic illness, which means (apart from God) there is no cure, although it can go into remission. The doctor said it was necessary to have rest, proper medication, and a minimum of stress.

Frankly, I was mad. I complained, "God, why now? I've given my children my best shot and now I want some time for *me*! And why *chronic*? Why not something that can be operated on, or radiated, or amputated? Why am I stuck with this body in rebellion?" I knew all the theology about living in an unredeemed world, and the effects of the curse on us all. I knew bad things happened to good people. But this was *me*, and it wasn't fair! I didn't want to be an invalid or "sickly." I had places to go, people to see, things to do. But my life had to change. I became acquainted with suffering and pain, and discovered that I was in a fellowship of millions. I was experiencing a common human problem. Again God spoke to me through His Word, this time from the writings of Peter. He gently chided, "Beloved, do not think it strange concerning the fiery trial which is to try you, as though some strange thing happened to you; but rejoice to the extent that you partake of Christ's sufferings, that when His glory is revealed, you may also be glad with exceeding joy" (1 Peter 4:12-13).

Other Scriptures ministered to me with breathtaking relevance. I understood anew that the Bible not only is a rich source of education, history and moral teaching, but also offers supernatural comfort to an aching and wondering heart.

I offer these studies to you out of my own experience with the confidence that God will speak to you, wherever you are in life. Many times I have been delighted and surprised to hear from a reader of the "In God's Word" column in *Virtue* magazine on how a particular study helped her, when that passage of Scripture had spoken to me in another way. That is further evidence of our Lord's intimate and loving care for each one of us, His children. No one knows you better or loves you more than our Lord does. I encourage you to let Him into your life through His Spirit-inspired Word.

Special thanks to Ruth Keller for faithfully editing each Bible study. Thanks too, to Bob Hawkins and Eileen Mason of Harvest House for their encouragement, and hugs to my wonderful husband, Bill, and children for their support.

AUTHOR'S NOTE

There have been many requests for these devotionals in book form. Some women who write me use *Virtue's* "In God's Word" column as an aid to their private devotional time. Some married couples do the studies together. Then there are other people who use the devotionals in a neighborhood or church Bible study group. Regardless of how you use the studies in this book, here are suggestions on how to get the most out of them:

1. *Read the suggested Scripture readings first.* Read the passages straight through, not stopping to check cross-references (you can do that later).

2. *Next, begin a careful examination of the passage.* Reread the Scripture meditatively and write answers to the questions under "Digging into the Details." You may wish to use an accompanying notebook.

3. *Respond to the mental stimulation of other questions or ideas this passage brings to mind under "Further Reflections."* Now is a good time to check cross-references. Make personal notes of thoughts that come to your attention.

4. *Finally, have the courage to pray,* "Lord, what are You saying to me through these Scriptures—and how can I respond?"

I

Daniel: Man of Conviction

෨

Esther: Woman of Influence

෨

The Dynamic Work of Faith

෨

The Story of Three Women

Daniel: Man of Conviction

Today's Theme: Having the courage of your convictions . . . "behaving" your beliefs.

Moments in Prayer: "Lord, our lives, attitudes and behavior can be wrongly influenced by our environment. We pray for renewed minds and self-discipline that will enable us to live what we believe. Amen."

Scripture Reading: Daniel 1–3.

To get the most out of your time in God's Word, after completing the Scripture readings in each devotional jot down ideas that are especially meaningful to you. Then come back to your notes later for further personal study.

Introductory Insights: Daniel, Hananiah, Mishael and Azariah were four young men who were taken captive from Judah to serve in Babylon, probably while still in their teens. They were the "cream of the crop"—good-looking, intelligent and discerning.

Babylon was a sophisticated city that was well-developed in language, literature and the sciences. Much of the feasting and sensual celebrations were centered around the worship of their gods. It was into this environment that these young Hebrew men were brought to serve the government officials.

Daniel developed into a competent leader and spent the rest of his life in Babylon as a government official *and* a prophet of the true God. Perhaps the key to Daniel's success is found in Daniel 1:8. "But Daniel purposed in his heart..." He was a man with great determination, commitment and self-discipline.

Digging into the Details:
1. *Read Daniel 1.*

A. What was the first test of the four young men in Babylon (verses 5-20)?

B. How did Daniel handle this challenge to his faith (verses 10-13)?

C. How does their response show creativity, and what were the results of their stand (verses 11-20)?

D. From their example, what can we learn about understanding and relating to our culture?

2. *Read Daniel 2.*

A. *Read verses 1-13.* Describe in your own words what is happening.

B. Notice how Daniel takes the initiative to defuse the matter (verses 14-16). How do his actions show leadership and assertiveness?

C. *Read verses 17-23.* What does this passage show of the importance these men placed on praying for one another?

D. What did Daniel do to help his "prayer partners" (verse 49)?

3. *Read Daniel 3.*

A. What evidence would suggest Nebuchadnezzar was a proud man (verses 1-7)?

B. Shadrach, Meshach and Abed-Nego had worked faithfully for Nebuchadnezzar for at least 15 years. How were they discredited by the astrologers or Chaldeans (verses 8-12)?

C. *Read verses 16-18*. These three courageous men did not know they would survive the fiery furnace, yet they had a stubborn faith. What can we learn from them?

D. What were the results of their standing up for their convictions (verses 28-30)?

E. *See Psalm 91:3-9 and Isaiah 43:2*. How do these verses encourage you?

Further Reflections: Shadrach, Meshach and Abed-Nego did not defend themselves, but *they knew what was right*. If they got thrown into the furnace, they knew God was able to save them. Even if they knew beforehand that God was not going to spare them, this wouldn't change their decision. They were not going to compromise their faith and bow to Nebuchadnezzar's image of gold (3:18).

We see that in chapter 6, Daniel knew that the consequences of his prayer life meant the lion's den. But consequences did not rule his life or form his convictions. These four men had faith—regardless! Hebrews 11 and Job 13:15 give further examples of faith.

Notice Daniel and his friends did not insist that those around them do what they believed was right, even though they had the power to enforce it. They simply were obedient to their own convictions and in following them, made an impact in Babylon.

Convictions turn into *condemnation* when we try to force others to live out our own convictions.

Points to Ponder:

❧ What if we simply follow our own convictions (assuming they're biblical)? A quiet "no" (or "yes," depending on the circumstances) followed up with resolve speaks volumes.

❧ What if our children were taken captive by ungodly people? Would we have built the Word and godly principles so strongly into their lives that they would lead committed, disciplined lives of faith?

Esther: Woman of Influence

Today's Theme: Esther's courageous response to opportunity.

Moments in Prayer: "Lord, show me through Esther's courageous example how I too can use opportunities to effect change for righteousness. Amen."

Scripture Reading: The Book of Esther.

Introductory Insights: The story of Esther takes place during the reign of King Ahasuerus—also known as Xerxes I—in Persia around 480 B.C. This is the resettlement and rebuilding period after Israel's defeat by Babylon.

During a grand feast, King Ahasuerus, drunk with wine, sends for Queen Vashti to appear before his guests—an unusual request for an Oriental king. She refuses. Because of his public humiliation by her refusal to appear, King Ahasuerus deposes Queen Vashti.

A new national beauty contest is held so that the king can choose a new queen. Esther, an orphaned Jewish girl being raised by her uncle Mordecai, enters the contest and wins.

Digging into the Details:

1. *The Main Characters: Ahasuerus, Mordecai, Haman, Esther*

A. What does the status of women appear to be during this time?

B. In reading the first two chapters of Esther, what is your impression of King Ahasuerus? How was he influenced (1:13-21; 2:1-4; 3:8-11)?

C. Marriage to Ahasuerus was probably not an emotionally intimate one. How do you think Esther handled the relationship (2:16-23; 5:1-8; and chapters 7 and 8)?

D. What difference did Mordecai make in the king's palace (2:4-17, 19-23; and chapters 4, 8 and 9)?

E. What kind of influence did Haman have upon Ahasuerus (chapter 3)?

2. *Seizing the Opportunity*

A. What were the opportunities that came Esther's way, and how did she use them (chapters 2, 4, 5, 7 and 8)?

B. Compare the "maneuvering" of Mordecai and Esther to that of Haman. How did their motivations differ?

C. What were the risks involved for Esther?

D. What possible risks do you face in opportunities that come your way?

Further Reflections: Esther possesses some unique qualities:

1. *She is a learner.* She listens to her Uncle Mordecai and also to advice given to her by advisors on how best to please the king.
2. *She is willing to take risks.* She risks failure in the initial beauty contest, and she risks death by going unbidden to the king.
3. *She is creative.* She uses whatever is at her disposal—her good looks, her position as queen to host banquets, her accessibility to the throne.
4. *She puts her best foot forward.* She has a flair for the dramatic. She knows how and when to take action and then uses wisdom and tact when doing so.

On a separate sheet of paper, write down your thoughts on how you can develop the above qualities in your own life.

Read Ephesians 5:1-21. A Sunday school song "This Little Light of Mine, I'm Gonna Let It Shine" tells an important truth. Sometimes things in life can cause us to give out a faltering or sputtering light. The *fear of man*—what others think of us—can blind our eyes to exciting possibilities that God has set before us.

Points to Ponder: Spend some time thinking about the unique sphere of influence that God has given you. Then write answers to these questions:

☙ What kind of influence do I have?

❧ What is my ultimate motivation in my influence?

❧ What practical difference does my life make in other people's lives?

❧ Am I so convinced of the principles of righteousness that I am quick to obey God rather than man?

The Dynamic Work of Faith

Faith says, "Trust and obey God."

Today's Theme: Faith

Moments in Prayer: *"Lord, how natural it is for us to depend on our world's wisdom and resources for solutions to life's challenges. But in doing so, we miss the exhilaration of faith—the reality of Your guidance . . . Your unexpected gifts . . . Your presence making a difference in our lives. Teach us what it means to 'walk by faith.' Amen."*

Scripture Reading: Hebrews 11; Hebrews 12:1,2; and James 2:14-26.

Introductory Insights: In Luke 18:8, Jesus asks this penetrating question: *"When the Son of Man comes, will He find faith on the earth?"* Jesus' return will occur as "in the days of Noah" (Luke 17) as people are eating, drinking, marrying and living life with no thought of eternity.

We too are involved with our world—the daily-ness of it, the business as usual. And we must be, to some degree. We work, play, raise our families.

But if we are people of faith, there is a difference. We see the "unseen"—the eternal. We are people with a future. Faith says, *"This isn't all there is."* Faith says, *"Listen; obey God* and watch the results." Faith says, *"Get your eyes off the circumstances and on the Almighty One."*

Jesus used the terms *faith* and *belief* interchangeably. Faith is belief in some person or thing. It is based on evidence, or testimony.

We have evidence of Jesus' presence in the world through God's Word and concrete facts. God didn't create us as intelligent, thinking people only to say, "All right now—jump into the dark." He gives us *illustrations* of faith.

Hebrews 11 lists some of the men and women who chose to believe God in spite of some overwhelming obstacles. We too can choose to believe Him.

Our belief, our faith, is a gift we can give God. And faith does its most dynamic work when we are pushed to the limits of our endurance. That's a perfect time to allow God to prove Himself as God.

Digging into the Details:

1. *Read Hebrews 11:1-31 and James 2:14-26.*

A. Rewrite in your own words the definition of faith (Hebrews 11:1-3).

B. Describe the kind of faith that pleases God (Hebrews 11:6 and James 2:14-26).

C. Reread Hebrews 11:8-32. How were these people influenced by their ancestors to have faith (Abraham to Isaac; Isaac to Jacob and Esau; Jacob to Joseph, etc.)?

D. Give a personal example of someone who inspired you to have more faith.

2. *Read Hebrews 11:13-16; 11:32-40; and Hebrews 12:1,2.*

A. Do you think it's harder to have faith when you don't see answers to prayer right away? If so, what can help you keep your perspective (11:13-16)?

B. From reading verses 32-40, does it appear to you that faith means getting what you want from God? Why or why not?

   C. After reading through Romans 11, the great "Hall of Fame" faith chapter, what significance do the first two verses of chapter 12 have?

   D. Think of someone—perhaps in your family—who died without seeing his or her prayers answered (Hebrews 11:13). Have you seen some of these prayers answered since? How can you pass on the legacy of faith in your family?

   Further Reflections: There are great benefits to living a life of faith. On a separate sheet of paper, look up these Scriptures and write down the *personal benefits* of faith.

Psalm 64:10	Psalm 84:12
Isaiah 26:3	Matthew 15:28
Acts 16:31	Proverbs 29:25
Psalm 40:4	John 7:38
Matthew 28:30	

   A Personal Illustration: My grandmother was widowed as a young woman after only eight years of marriage. Alone, she raised four children during the Depression. She had no income, and there was no Social Security. Just to have rent money and food on the table took daily faith and hard work. She knew what it meant to prove God.

I remember when I was small, my grandmother would often sing this hymn:

> 'Tis so sweet to trust in Jesus, Just to take Him at His word;
> Just to rest upon His promise; Just to know 'thus saith the Lord.'
> Jesus, Jesus, how I trust Him, How I've proved Him o'er and o'er.
> Jesus, Jesus, precious Jesus! O for grace to trust Him more."
>
> —*William J. Kirkpatrick*

Now here I am, two generations later. My pantry is full; refrigerator stocked; we have a steady income. And yet God has proved Himself to me as a woman, a wife and mother so many times. Ours is a generation full of stress, mind-games, subtle and not-so-subtle temptations. If ever there is a time when we have an opportunity to trust God, to grow in faith, it is today.

Points to Ponder:

🕊 What do I need faith for in my life right now?

🕊 Who—or what—is the object of my faith?

🕊 What kind of faith heritage am I leaving for my children?

The Story of Three Women

Ruth responded to life with love.

Today's Theme: Examining the different responses to life in three women: Ruth, Orpah and Naomi.

Moments in Prayer: *"Lord, show me through Ruth's life how I may further develop the character traits of loyalty and commitment. Amen."*

Scripture Reading: The Book of Ruth.

Introductory Insights: The story is set in the period of the Book of Judges. It was a time of spiritual decline marked by weak faith and irresponsible conduct. There was an attitude of permissiveness: "In those days there was no king in Israel; everyone did what was right in his own eyes" (Judges 21:25).

Ruth becomes an even more remarkable person as you realize her background: She was a descendant of the Moabites, a nation that originated from the incestuous relations that Lot's daughters had with their father.

Digging into the Details:

Naomi: In the prime of her life, everything she holds dear is taken from her. Even hope is gone, as she has no grandsons to carry on her family line. This is the ultimate tragedy in her culture. What are some clues to Naomi's feelings of self-worth (Ruth 1:8,11-13)?

What was Naomi's attitude toward Ruth and Orpah?

What was Naomi's attitude toward God (Ruth 2:20,21)?

Orpah: From the brief verses in chapter 1 that describe Orpah, how do you think she felt toward Naomi?

A lot of us have good intentions. But when we're faced with an unpleasant situation and a person with a martyr spirit such as Naomi's, it's easy to run the other way. Put yourself in Orpah's place. What would you have done?

Ruth: Ruth's and Orpah's losses were equally great. Why do you think Ruth was determined to stay with her mother-in-law?

Read again Ruth 1:16-18 and Ruth 2–3 and write a paragraph that describes how you visualize Ruth's character and personality.

What are some clues to Ruth's feelings of self-worth?

Do you think Naomi appreciated Ruth's commitment at first?

What was her attitude toward Ruth later (Ruth 4:14-17)?

We meet Boaz, the "kinsman-redeemer" in chapter 2. What kind of man was Boaz? (Ruth 2–4).

What kind of marriage do you think Ruth and Boaz had? Why?

How does this story show the provision of God, and how can you apply it personally?

Further Reflections: What a lovely person Ruth was! She seemed to be able to love with strong love, regardless of the response. She was able to do what needed to be done—quietly and without fanfare. She lived responsibly before God, and God abundantly rewarded her.

We're left with a warm feeling from this story because it has a happy ending: Ruth marries a wonderful man who cares for her, and Naomi's arms are no longer empty but full with a beautiful baby boy.

Points to Ponder:

❧ Do I accept God's love for me so that I am able to love the way Ruth did?

❧ Are there times in my life when, like Orpah, I walk away from a situation?

❧ Is my trust for God like Ruth's? Can I simply be obedient to Him and trust Him for the result?

II

Determining Priorities

Who's First in My Life?

&

Finding God's Will

&

Building for Eternity

&

Who Owns Me?

&

The Trap of Materialism

Who's First in My Life?

Today's Theme: Placing God first in our lives over every other "god" (money, ambition, possessions, people or pleasure).

Moments in Prayer: *"Lord, as we examine our lives, we ask that You will be Lord of all. Show us anything that would detract from having You be first. Amen."*

Scripture Reading: Joshua 24:1-24 and Matthew 6:19-24.

Introductory Insights: In the passage from Joshua, we see Joshua as an old man about to die. He had seen great things done by Jehovah God for the children of Israel.

After spending 40 years in the wilderness, Joshua had been chosen by God to be Israel's leader. He took them across the Jordan River into the Promised Land, around the walls of Jericho and through the land of Canaan, defeating the enemies of Israel and possessing the land that God had promised to them through Abraham and Moses.

Now he stood before the people for the last time, with grave concern. His concern was caused by the fact that while Israel occupied the Promised Land now, not all of their enemies had been defeated.

But the people of Israel were tired of fighting their enemies, and they had become content to cohabitate with them instead. Because the enemy was not pressing them, they would not press the enemy.

Joshua had already seen how the gods of the enemy were being worshiped by some Israelites. He saw the potential compromise at hand through intermarriage and acceptance of pagan gods. And so with great conviction and resolve, he reminds the people of God's leadership out of Egypt, through the Red Sea, in the defeat of Israel's enemies and on into the Promised Land. Further, he challenges them to "choose this day whom you will serve."

Digging into the Details:

1. *Read Joshua 24:1-12*. What was God trying to emphasize by this narration?

2. *Read Joshua 24:13*. What is God trying to emphasize in this verse and how could its principles apply to you personally?

3. *Read Joshua 24:14-24*.

　　A. How many times does Joshua challenge the children

of Israel to serve Jehovah God and how many times did they respond?

B. Why do you think Joshua was not satisfied with their first response and made them repeat their commitment?

C. Note verse 15 in particular. What challenge does Joshua present to the people of Israel?

4. *Read Matthew 6:19-24.*

A. How do you interpret the meaning of verses 19-23?

B. How does verse 24 relate to what Joshua was saying?

Further Reflections: John Newton, who was a slave trader before his conversion to Christ, had a favorite verse that he wrote in large letters and hung over his mantelpiece: "Remember that you were a slave in the land of Egypt and that the Lord your God redeemed you" (Deuteronomy 15:15).

Whether we study the Old Testament or the New, you and I are continually reminded that we are not Christians because of a long, wise and godly heritage. We come from rebellion. Individually we are sinners, children of wrath.

After we become Christians, we must look at others who are still under sin's bondage and say, "I am essentially what they are. If I am now redeemed, it is not because I am intrinsically better but because God, by His grace, has done a work in my life."

Every household, every parent, every individual must choose daily to put God first. The challenge of Joshua to "choose this day whom you will serve" should confront us often as we make decisions. Joshua's response should be quick to come from our own hearts and lips: "As for me and my house, we will serve the Lord."

Points to Ponder:

🕿 The idols of ancient times were pagan statues of false gods. List some of the "idols" of our day.

🕿 Take a sheet of paper and divide it in half. On one side list your priorities as they currently are, and on the other side list them as you feel God wants them to be in your life.

   Be sure to include all of the things that use up your time, including work, family, church, recreation, school, devotional time, pursuit of pleasure, watching television, taking care of/using possessions and ministering to others.

Finding God's Will

Today's Theme: Finding God's will in complex situations

Moments in Prayer: *"Lord, show us how to wait upon You for the right answers. Thank You for reminding us in Scripture that it is 'not by might, nor by power, but by [Your] Spirit' that mountains are moved. Amen."*

Scripture Reading: 2 Chronicles 17–20. (There is more reading than usual in this study, so you may wish to divide this into two studies: chapters 17–18; and chapters 19–20.)

Introductory Insights: Jehoshaphat, king of Judah in 873 B.C., was a good leader. He was not perfect—he made mistakes—but he was sincere in wanting to follow God and lead his people in God's ways (2 Chronicles 17). He earned the respect of his people and even of his enemies, and became prosperous. He built up his kingdom by sending out teachers to teach the law of the Lord to all the cities of Judah. Second Chronicles 17:10 says ". . . the fear of the Lord fell on all the kingdoms of the lands that were around Judah."

In 2 Chronicles 18 we see that Jehoshaphat makes an alliance with King Ahab (husband of Jezebel), king of Israel. We are told in 2 Kings 8:16-18 that they were related by the marriage of Jehoshaphat's son to Ahab and Jezebel's daughter, which later opened the door to Baal worship in Judah.

In chapter 18, we see a remarkable exchange between Jehoshaphat and Ahab. Jehoshaphat was paying a state visit to Ahab, who had provided an enormous barbecue for the occasion. Ahab asked Jehoshaphat to go with him to war against Ramoth Gilead to reclaim the land. As his ally, Jehoshaphat reaffirmed his support, but then asked, "Please inquire for the word of the Lord today" (18:4). Ahab called his staff of 400 prophets who told him what he wanted to hear: "Go for it, Ahab—you'll win." Jehoshaphat was not satisfied with that answer and asked Ahab if he didn't have another prophet of God (someone evidently not on Ahab's payroll). Ahab reluctantly brought out Micaiah, whom he disliked because, as he complained to Jehoshaphat, "He never prophecies good concerning me, but always evil."

Chapter 19 briefly describes a confrontation that Jehu had with Jehoshaphat over his unholy alliance with Ahab, then details the reforms that Jehoshaphat instituted in Judah. Chapter 20:1-30 tells the astounding miracle of Jehoshaphat's victory and the unusual tactics that the Lord told him to use.

Digging into the Details:
1. *Read 2 Chronicles 17–18.*

A. Why do you think Jehoshaphat was a successful king?

B. List some positive things he did to lead his nation (17:1-12).

C. How do you know that Jehoshaphat wanted to find God's will (18:1-7)?

D. What did Ahab find offensive about Micaiah, and how did he treat him (18:7-27)?

E. Why do you think it is hard for us to hear the truth about ourselves?

2. *Read 2 Chronicles 19.*

A. Why is it unwise to make alliances with the ungodly (see 19:1-3; and 2 Corinthians 6:14-18)?

B. We read in 19:4-11 of the second revival in Jehoshaphat's reign. What insights could someone in leadership gain from his example?

C. How can you apply facts from chapter 19 to your own spiritual leadership of your family?

3. *Read 2 Chronicles 20.*

A. What was the bad news that Jehoshaphat received, and what was his reaction (verses 1-13)?

B. Describe a time when you or someone close to you faced what seemed to be an overwhelming problem.

C. Detail God's clear instructions to Jehoshaphat, and the results (verses 14-30). (Use a separate sheet of paper, if necessary.)

D. How could you apply the instructions given to Jehoshaphat to your own circumstances?

Further Reflections: The "high places" referred to in 2 Chronicles 15:16,17; 17:6; and 20:33 were *asherah*, a pillar or image of wood set up with the image of Baal. They were worshiped with perverted, sensual rituals in demonic orgies. Jehoshaphat gave orders in his "housecleaning" of Judah to have these removed. Either they were removed and later rebuilt, or his orders were never fully carried out, because we see in verse 33 of chapter 20 that ". . . *the high places were not taken away, for as yet the people had not directed their hearts to the God of their fathers.*" What went wrong here? Perhaps the key to the continued pockets of idolatry was a divided heart. This, as well as the bad alliances that Jehoshaphat made, is a jarring note in an otherwise victorious story. And yet it makes these men and women of Scripture all the more real. We all have our vulnerabilities, our weaknesses. We all have "high places" that we must be determined to clean out.

A comforting thought: We consistently see in Scripture that when God's people turned from their sins back to God, He always met them with open arms. We see in Jehoshaphat a beautiful illustration of the personal love and guidance that God will show us if we are willing to listen.

Points to Ponder: In my life am I careful to:

?? Guard against unequal alliances (although it may be convenient)?

❧ Seek God's will carefully (even if it's unpopular)?

❧ Speak God's truth (even if it hurts)?

❧ Follow God's leading, because *"the battle is not yours, but God's"* (2 Chronicles 20:15)?

Building for Eternity

Our lives take on the shape of who we are.

Today's Theme: Wise building

Moments in Prayer: *"Lord, daily we build our lives by our choices, actions and responses. We pray for discernment to make choices that draw us closer to You, the solid Rock. Amen."*

Scripture Reading: Luke 6:46-49; Luke 14:26-35; 1 Corinthians 3:9-17; John 3:1-21; and Mark 10:17-31.

Introductory Insights: Have you ever driven by a house where you used to live? Recently I drove by a little house where my husband and I lived over 20 years ago. The house looked vaguely familiar, but it wasn't home. It certainly was much smaller than I had remembered. The rosebushes were overgrown, the weeds flourished and the house needed paint. It was a rental and obviously had housed a string of temporary inhabitants on their way to—hopefully—something better.

Houses tend to take on the personalities of the people who live in them. On my way to the office, I pass a home that is very attractively kept. It is warm, inviting, welcoming. I don't know the inhabitants, yet I appreciate what I see and can almost visualize stopping by for coffee and a chat.

Our lives are like houses: They take on the shape of who we are. (Remember, however: First-time impressions *can* be misleading—you may change your mind once inside the front door!)

I have a friend who is a new believer in Christ. She cheerfully admits that her whole family is under massive reconstruction. These kinds of projects take time and are often messy as we muddle through them. But if we stick to the plan, order and beauty eventually emerge.

Jesus talked about the wise man who built his house on a rock. And in Proverbs 14:1 we read of the wise woman who builds her house versus the foolish one who tears hers down.

This study deals with the necessary ingredients of building: 1. The Plan, 2. The Foundation, and 3. The Materials.

Digging into the Details:

1. "The Plan." *Read John 3:1-21; Luke 14:26-33; and Mark 10:17-31.*

A. From reading John 3:1-21, describe in your own words how an individual can come to new life in Christ. (Don't use evangelical "buzz" words—explain as though you are talking to someone who knows nothing of the Gospel.)

B. *Read Luke 14:26-33.* What does this passage say to you about being a follower of Christ?

C. What do you believe it means to "count the cost" of being a disciple (see verses 28-33)?

D. *Read Mark 10:17-31.* What was the cost of following Jesus to this young man? Do you believe that wealth is the issue here? Why or why not?

E. How would you "count the cost" of building a marriage, of raising a family, of a particular commitment?

2. "The Foundation." *Read Luke 6:46-49 and 1 Peter 2:4-12.*

A. What do the above Scriptures say about what we should build our lives upon?

B. From reading the story of the wise man in Luke 6, why is the foundation so important?

C. What do these Scriptures have to say about account-
ability to Scripture and to the body of Christ? Who is the
chief Cornerstone?

3. "The Materials." *Read 1 Corinthians 3:9-17; Proverbs
14:1; Jude 20; and 1 Thessalonians 5:11.*

A. See 1 Corinthians 3:9-17. What does this passage say
about building into our lives things that really matter?

B. In reading Proverbs 14:1, in what ways does the wise
woman *build* her house? What different things in your life
could this apply to (see also Jude 20)? Apply this Scripture
both spiritually and then practically.

C. What about the foolish woman who *tears* her house
down "with her own hands" (Proverbs 14:1)? In what ways
can we also be destructive about our lives?

D. How can we be instrumental in helping others build their lives (see 1 Thessalonians 5:11)?

Further Reflections: Living godly lives doesn't just happen. We live in a fallen world—weeds take over and dust collects. Things rot, decay. The natural bent is downward. That's why it is essential that we use our God-given choice to make Christ the Cornerstone of our lives and to follow the plan that He has set out for us in Scripture.

The definition of "building" is to "create by forming and combining materials; to give form to, according to a definite plan or process." God has given each of us a unique "house." You have something to contribute that no one else can. Read in 2 Kings 4:1-7 about the widow who used what she had: a meager supply of oil.

For further study about the treasures that we have in our houses, read Proverbs 15:6 and 8:20,21. On a separate sheet of paper, list the treasures that you have in your life (some you may have overlooked!).

Points to Ponder:

ஐ What do I have in my house and in my life?

ஐ In what ways can I consciously build into my life the things that last?

ஐ How can I encourage growth in those close to me?

Who Owns Me?

Love for the world leaves no room for Jesus.

Today's Theme: Loving God or loving the world.

Moments in Prayer: *"Lord, show me through this study how I can love You with all my heart, soul and mind. Amen."*

Scripture Reading: Matthew 22:37-40; Matthew 16:24-26; 1 John 2:15-17; Matthew 6:24.

Digging into the Details:
1. *Loving the World.*

   A. From Scripture we understand that it is not possible to "love God" and "love the world" at the same time. What does it mean to "love the world" (1 John 2:15-17)?

   B. Look up and write down any additional insights you have about these temptations:
   ᴥ *Lust of the flesh*—Galatians 5:19-21.

50

❧ *Lust of the eyes*—Genesis 3:6 (Eve's fall) and 2 Samuel 11 (David's fall).

❧ *Pride of life*—Ezekiel 28:17 (Satan's fall).

C. Describe any parallels you see between the above temptations and Jesus' temptation in the wilderness in Matthew 4:1-11.

D. In what way did Jesus defeat Satan?

E. How can we defeat Satan? (See Revelation 12:11; Hebrews 4:12; Romans 12:1-2.)

2. *Loving God.*

A. What does it mean to "love God"? (See John 14:15; Matthew 22:37-40; Matthew 16:24-26.)

B. Matthew 22:37-41 says you shall love God with all your *heart* (all inward affections); all your *soul* (all consciousness) and all your *mind* (all thoughts). What practical difference will it make in your life to love God this way?

The tragedy of "loving the world" is that love for the world leaves no room for Jesus.

Jesus says in Matthew 16:26, "What is a man profited if he gains the whole world, and loses his own soul?" An empty profit, indeed.

On the other hand, when we are consumed with loving God with all our heart, soul and mind, and our neighbor as ourselves, our lives become filled and directed by the Holy Spirit. We are able to resist temptation through Jesus' name (James 4:4-10).

Further Reflections:

A. We must be careful when we begin labeling what is "worldly" and what is not. Paul the apostle wrote of the early Christians debating whether or not it was right to eat meat that had been offered to idols. (Read Romans 14.) What advice did Paul give? (See Romans 14:3-4,10-21; Romans 15:1; 1 Corinthians 10:31-33.)

B. How can you apply these principles?

C. Now go back to the list of things that impressed you about the original passages in the "Reading" section. Find key words and thoughts in those verses. If you have a cross-reference Bible, there will be other references in the margin that will give you additional insights.

If you have a concordance, look up other passages with key words that refer to the same subject. Most importantly, spend time meditating on these passages.

Points to Ponder:

❧ How am I expressing love for God?

❧ Am I able to successfully live *in* the world yet not be *of* the world?

❧ What motivates me? What are my goals?

❧ Who "owns" me?

❧ Whom or what do I love most of all?

> O Love that wilt not let me go,
>   I rest my weary soul in Thee.
> I give Thee back the life I owe
>   That in Thine ocean depths its flow
>   May richer, fuller be.
>   —George Matheson

The Trap of Materialism

Today's Theme: Seeing covetousness for what it is: a temporary, vain attempt to satisfy eternal hunger.

Moments in Prayer: *"Lord, so fill our vision that we will have complete rest and fulfillment in knowing You, the all-sufficient One. Amen."*

Scripture Reading: Hebrews 13:5,6; Luke 12:15-34; Joshua 7; James 1:13-15; Genesis 3; 2 Samuel 11.

"You shall not covet . . ." (Exodus 20:17).

"Let your conduct be without covetousness, and be content with such things as you have. For He Himself has said, *'I will never leave you nor forsake you.'* So we may boldly say: 'The Lord is my helper; I will not fear. What can man do to me?' " (Hebrews 13:5,6).

Introductory Insights: The dictionary defines covetousness as "being excessively desirous of the possessions of another; marked by extreme desire to acquire or possess." We live in a world that promotes covetousness. Appealing advertising campaigns and easy credit make it possible to have it all—now.

Never have we lived so well, yet the drive for more is

relentless. Better houses, cars, clothing, vacations, etc. The desire to "possess" the ideal lover (regardless if he or she is married to someone else) is popularly sanctioned by modern role models, current movies, TV and novels. If you like it, take it.

Coveting is not new. It's as old as the Garden of Eden when Eve yielded to the forbidden fruit. It's as old as the stories of Achan (Joshua 7) and of David's coveting Bathsheba (2 Samuel 11). Jesus warned against covetousness because of the disastrous traps it holds.

Digging into the Details:
1. *Read Luke 12:15-34.*

A. See verses 17-19. What do you think was the motivation for the rich man's actions?

B. Why was his scheme pointless (verses 20-21)?

C. Read the rest of the passage carefully. What does verse 23 mean to you personally?

2. Read Joshua 7; 2 Samuel 11; Genesis 3.

A. Why did the children of Israel get defeated at Ai (Joshua 7:10-12)?

B. How does one sin lead to another (Joshua 7:20-21)?

C. Achan, King David and Adam and Eve all tried in various ways to cover their sin. What were their methods and why was it impossible to do (Joshua 7; 2 Samuel 11; Genesis 3)?

3. Read James 1:12-16.

A. What is the difference between "temptation" and "covetousness"?

It is not a sin to be tempted. Jesus was tempted. Coveting is the "second look," the determined, "I-want-that-regardless-of-what-happens" attitude.

We all have it in us to covet. Because of our personal, individual weaknesses, we are drawn to satisfy certain appetites. When Jesus said, "Beware of covetousness," He was telling us to be on guard against our fallen natures. None of us can afford spiritual pride and say, "It could never happen to me."

Pascal said, "We can only know God well when we know our own sin. And those who have known God without knowing their wretchedness have not glorified Him, but have glorified themselves."

Paul said in Romans 7:24-25, "O wretched man that I am! Who will deliver me from this body of death? I thank God— through Jesus Christ our Lord!"

Further Reflections:

A. *Read Genesis 28:15-17 and Joshua 1:5-7.* God gives both Jacob and Joshua assurances of His constant presence: *"I will never leave you nor forsake you."* In your opinion, what was the significance of this promise?

B. Has there been a time in your life when you especially needed to hear this promise from God? Describe the circumstances.

C. How can this promise liberate us from materialism? From trying to please people? From fear? From covetousness?

Points to Ponder:

❧ Is it possible that putting my security in "things" is masking spiritual hunger that only God can satisfy?

❧ Do I know God so thoroughly, so intimately that I can honestly say, *"The Lord is my helper; I will not fear"* (Hebrews 13:6)?

> Riches I need not,
> nor man's empty praise,
> Thou mine inheritance,
> now and always;
> Thou and Thou only,
> first in my heart,
> High King of Heaven,
> my Treasure Thou art.
> —Mary Byrne

III

Nurturing Relationships

Learning to Love

❧

Healing Friendships

❧

Rash Judgments

❧

When Love Turns Sour

❧

Relinquishment—
Key to Blessing

Learning to Love

God's love is demon- strated by action.

Today's Theme: Understanding, accepting and giving God's love.

Moments in Prayer: *"Lord, help us to understand how great and all-encompassing Your love is. Help us to realize Your intimate care for us. And then, Lord, show us how we can love others the way You love us. Amen."*

Scripture Reading: 1 Corinthians 13; 1 John.

Digging into the Details:
1. *Defining love.*

Love is an overused word. We use it to describe the mundane to the profound. But God's love, agape love, is not just an emotional tug of the heart. "Agape," the Greek word for love, corresponds to the Hebrew covenantal term "hesed," which describes the spiritual concern that God had for His chosen people of Israel when He showed His provisional care for them. God showed us, fallen mankind, His self-sacrificing love by seeing our need for redemption and giving us Jesus to die on the cross for us and take our sins away.

God's love is demonstrated by action. God saw our need and

met it. He loved us before we were capable of loving in return. (See 1 John 4:9-10 and John 3:16.)

"But God commended His love toward us, in that, while we were yet sinners, Christ died for us" (Romans 5:8 KJV). Another word for "commended" is "proved." God proved His love for us by giving us Jesus.

2. Applying God's love.

Read 1 John 1:5-10; 2:1-3. What do these Scriptures say about the importance of recognizing our need of God's redeeming love?

The pivotal point in all of our lives must be this very fact: We cannot stand before a holy God on our own merit. It is only through confessing our sin and acknowledging our need of a Savior that we become accepted in the "Beloved" (Ephesians 1:6-7; Psalm 32:5).

3. Loving with God's love.

See 1 John 4:11-21. When we know we are loved, we are liberated to love others. What keeps us from loving? Fear. Fear of rejection, fear of losing control, fear of being hurt again.

A God-directed love is one that loves regardless of the response. Jesus' sacrifice on the cross has been rejected by many, yet His love continues to reach for us.

List some thoughts on "loving others." How can you love your family, friends and those around you with agape love?

Further Reflections: Here is an illustration taken from *Walking on Water* by Madeleine L'Engle: "My son-in-law, Alan Jones, told me a story of a Hasidic rabbi, renowned for his piety. He was unexpectedly confronted one day by one of his devoted youthful disciples. In a burst of feeling, the young disciple exclaimed, 'My master, I love you!'

"The ancient teacher looked up from his books and asked his fervent disciple, 'Do you know what hurts me, my son?'

"The young man was puzzled. Composing himself he stuttered, 'I don't understand your question, Rabbi. I am trying to tell you how much you mean to me and you confuse me with irrelevant questions.'

" 'My question is neither confusing nor irrelevant,' rejoined the rabbi, 'for if you do not know what hurts me, how can you truly love me?' "*

We have a High Priest who is touched by the feeling of our infirmities. He *knows* what hurts us (Hebrews 4:14-16). He has borne our griefs and carried our sorrows (Isaiah 53:5-6).

We love others with agape love when we are able to look past the fault—sin—and see the need.

Make a personal love evaluation for the next month. Use a small notebook and write down insights from this passage. Measure your responses to family, friends and others by 1 Corinthians 13. Remember that love is action that meets needs. Keep in mind the source of all love.

---

* Taken from the *Disciplines of the Inner Life*, by Bob and Michael W. Benson, Word Books, 1985, p. 309. Originally from *Walking on Water: Reflections on Faith and Art*, Crosswick-Harold Shaw Publishers, Wheaton, Illinois, 1980.

Healing Friendships

Today's Theme: Bearing each other's burden and thus fulfilling the law of Christ.

Moments in Prayer: *"Thank You, Lord, for the gift of friendship. Show me ways to love and encourage my friends. Amen."*

Scripture Reading: Luke 10:25-37; Galatians 6:1-4; Romans 12:9-16.

Digging into the Details:
1. *Reread Luke 10:25-37.*

A. Who should have met the needs of the wounded man? List some of the probable reasons that kept the priest and Levite from getting involved with the wounded man.

B. The Jews and the Samaritans were intensely prejudiced against each other and kept their distance. What hinders us today from getting involved in other people's lives?

C. In what practical ways did the Good Samaritan show love, and how can we show love in practical ways to the "wounded" among us today?

2. *Reread Galatians 6:1-4.*

A. What similarities do you see between Paul's words and Jesus' parable in Luke 10:25-37?

B. What is an important ingredient to successfully restoring someone who has fallen? (See Galatians 6:1.)

C. Galatians 6:2 says, "Bear one another's burdens, and so fulfill the law of Christ." What is the "law of Christ," and how can you fulfill it? (See John 13:34-35.)

Further Reflections: Nothing will make you more sensitive to someone's problems than if you've been there before yourself. God has forgiven and restored *us*, so how can we withhold forgiveness, restoration and mercy from another person?

1. Think about the words "healing" and "restoration." Jot down some things that are necessary for healing.

2. Restoring an old piece of furniture involves loving, patient care and hard muscle work. But the result is always worth it—a beautiful and valuable keepsake to cherish. List some specific people and situations where you can help promote healing and restoration (i.e., broken relationships, church or employment problems or conflicts with friends and family).

3. What about your own hurts? The simple act of asking for and receiving prayer gives strength and makes the load easier. Sharing burdens is a two-way street.

If you are honest, loving and forgiving with others, you will receive honesty, love and forgiveness from them. How can you become more open with others about your needs?

4. Read Ecclesiastes 4:9-12. These verses point out how important friends are. Going it alone is hard, unnecessary and not scriptural.

We need Christian friends who will pray with us, tell us the truth and be loyal. What are some ways you can develop such friends? (See Proverbs 17:17; 18:24; 27:6; James 5:16 and Romans 12:9-16.)

5. Now go back to the list of things that impressed you about the original passages in the "Reading" section. Find key words and thoughts in those verses.

Points to Ponder:

ᔢ Have you noticed ways, big or small, that you have been able to bear burdens or encourage others?

ᔢ Have you spotted any prejudices in your life toward others that have made you insensitive to their wounds?

ᔢ What about the possibility of taking on some new prayer projects? Through prayer, you can help promote healing and restoration to those close to you. Don't worry about having to have all the answers. You only need to listen, to pray and to believe with others for God's answers.

Rash Judgments

Today's Theme: Looking behind the obvious situation for the "real story" and learning not to jump to conclusions.

Moments in Prayer: *"Lord, give us patience and discipline to not make immediate accusations or snap judgments against others, even though there is incriminating evidence. . . . Help us, Father, to see others through the eyes of Your love. Amen."*

Scripture Reading: Joshua 22 and John 12:1-8.

Introductory Insights: The opening part of Joshua 22 deals with the tribes of Reuben, Gad, and the half-tribe of Manasseh. They are crossing back over the Jordan to where their land lies, the portion that was given them by Moses.

They had left their families and flocks there seven years before, with some men to guard them. Joshua instructed them during the farewell to take with them the wealth they had gained from conquering cities in Canaan. It must have been difficult to say goodbye to their comrades-in-arms with whom they had shared many battles and victories.

They had seen God do many miracles for them. The Jordan

was indeed a barrier—there were no bridges in those days over the deep water—so the parting was quite final.

Digging into the Details:
1. *Read Joshua 22:9-12.*

    A. What did these 2¹/₂ tribes do upon leaving Canaan?

    B. What was the reaction of the 9¹/₂ tribes west of the Jordan?

2. *Read Joshua 22:13-20.*

    A. What did they actually do to handle this *supposed* rebellion against God?

3. *Read Joshua 22:21-34.*

    A. This story has a happy ending because this problem

was handled *correctly*. Describe the explanation that the tribes east of Jordan gave for building the altar.

A Personal Illustration: Some years ago my son had a teacher whom I judged to be a very cold person. She was efficient and did her job well, but she rarely smiled and went about her work in a detached, aloof manner. I secretly nicknamed her the "Ice Lady." Then I made a chance discovery.

This teacher had a grown son who was very ill with cystic fibrosis. She had watched her much-loved son grow into young adulthood knowing he could not live long. Her detached manner became a coping mechanism for dealing with this tragic situation.

It was a good lesson for me. How can I possibly judge what is in another's heart, or why a person behaves the way he or she does? How can I judge another's motivation, especially before I know the whole story?

Further Reflections:
1. *Read John 12:1-8.*

   A. What was Judas' reaction to Mary's extravagance?

B. His comments and attitude did not deter Mary from her worship and love for Jesus. What can we learn from Mary?

2. Appearances can be deceiving. We have all been misunderstood at some time or other for something we said or did. It hurts, and it's frustrating as well because we don't always get the chance to set the record straight. What should we do with those unresolved feelings?

Jesus was misunderstood and misjudged many times. But that didn't stop Him from doing the will of the Father or from loving and forgiving the very ones who were misjudging Him.

Points to Ponder: Go back over your original notes on Joshua 22 and John 12:1-8.

❧ Have you seen occasions where you have been able to extend understanding, mercy and compassion because of your willingness not to make rash judgments?

❧ How does *listening* to someone often give us a new perspective?

When Love Turns Sour

Forgiveness is a necessary part of love.

Today's Theme: How to keep disappointments from stifling love.

Moments in Prayer: *"Lord, I ask for an understanding of Your love. Thank You for loving me just for who I am right now. I pray for healing of past hurts and ask that love and joy will replace bitterness as I forgive. Amen."*

Scripture Reading: 1 Samuel 18:20-35; 19:8-17; 25:44; 2 Samuel 3:12-16; 6:12-23.

Introductory Insights: We will concentrate our study on the relationship of two people—David and Michal. As the story opens, we see a young couple with "stars" in their eyes. They are enamored by what they see in each other. Michal loves David, and David is honored to win the hand of the king's beautiful daughter. But all does not end happily ever after.

Saul makes life unbearable for David. Aided by Michal, David has to flee at night through a window. During David's exile, Saul married Michal off to another man—a slap in the face to David. Time passes.

After Saul's death and David's coronation, one of the first

things David demands is that Michal be brought back to him. Michal is torn from her home, and her second husband follows her, weeping. He evidently cared a great deal for her.

Next we see Michal watching David as he leads a procession into the city. They are bringing the Ark of the Covenant back, and David is filled with joy. Instead of sharing in the celebration, Michal looks at David with contempt and disgust. When David comes up to bless his household, Michal cuts him down with sarcastic words. The last record of Michal is: "Therefore Michal the daughter of Saul had no children to the day of her death" (2 Samuel 6:23).

Digging into the Details:

1. Try to imagine yourself in Michal's situation. What do you think had happened within her to cause her love for David to turn to contempt?

2. Do you think David deserved Michal's contempt? Why or why not?

3. What forces were at work around them that hurt their love relationship?

4. Do you see any way that their relationship could have been salvaged? How?

5. Which of the two do you believe suffered the most from this torn relationship, David or Michal? Why?

Further Reflections: We often have a false sense of love. We try to earn it in various ways, or we use our love to reward others for their actions. This is not the reason for God's love for us. He loved us while we were sinners (1 John 4:10). God's love is offered freely to us, and we hold the option of response. But the risk of love is rejection, and the greater your love, the more likely you are to be hurt.

We live in a fallen world. No one is perfect. Someday, sometime you will offend someone or someone may offend you. Lewis Smedges said, "We Christians tend to abridge the truth. Our theology does not allow for flawed or scarred Christians." *Forgiveness is a necessary component of love.*

Read Ephesians 4 and Matthew 18:15-35. Put into your own words what these passages have to say about forgiveness in relationships. Also read Hebrews 12:14-15, 28-29. When we do not forgive, bitterness begins to grow. Study these verses carefully to see the key to overcoming bitterness.

Points to Ponder:

🔊 Think of an instance in your life when love went sour for you. It could be a marriage, friendship, family or church situation. What destructive forces allowed this to happen?

🔊 If you could, would you change the way you responded? If so, how?

🔊 Now consider when a damaged relationship was healed and love remained. What made the difference?

Relinquishment— Key to Blessing

Today's Theme: Learning to let go.

Moments in Prayer: *"Lord, we care for so many things and people. Sometimes we get possessive and hold onto those things, even when they are Yours. Teach us the freedom in giving all to You. Amen."*

Scripture Reading: Genesis 22:1-18; 1 Samuel 15:1-35; 1 Samuel 1; 2:1-11, 2:18-21.

Introductory Insights: God promised Abraham that he would be the father of a great nation and of many sons. Unfortunately, Abraham and Sarah reached old age and still had no children.

Finally, after Abraham and Sarah had tried their own methods that were not in God's plan, God sent Isaac—the son of promise. In Genesis 22, we see a dramatic account of how God tested Abraham's obedience. Abraham had made plenty of mistakes over the years, but he had learned one thing: A close walk with God required obedience.

In 1 Samuel 15, there is a tragic story of King Saul's disobedience. Saul was talented, handsome, wealthy and powerful—but he lost it all.

In 1 Samuel 1–2, we read a poignant story of a mother who gave her best. When you read the stories of these three people, think about the temptation we as Christians have to wrap ourselves around another person, position, thing—even "ministry."

The individuals and things that we care about so deeply can become a crutch or security blanket to us. Our identity can get all tangled up in people and things instead of being rooted in God.

Here are some helpful definitions: To "possess" means "to hold onto; to have the use or benefit of; to dominate the mind or thoughts." "Possessive" is "a tendency to control or dominate; fearful of the loss of position or affection." "Relinquish" is "to let something go; abandon; surrender; waive rights. To give up a possession or claim."

It takes courage and determination to follow Christ. The good news is that God pours out His blessings on His children and never leaves them destitute. *We can trust Him.*

Digging into the Details:
1. *Read Genesis 22:1-18*

A. From reading this passage, how do you think Abraham felt toward Isaac?

B. *Read verses 5-8.* Describe the ways Abraham demonstrated faith in God.

C. *See verses 15-18.* What were the results of Abraham's obedience?

D. What are some natural reasons for Abraham to be possessive of Isaac?

E. Has there been an "Isaac" in your life? If so, describe the situation and your response.

2. *Read 1 Samuel 15:1-35.*

A. From reading this passage, what seems to be Saul's motivation for disobedience?

B. How did Saul use his influence and power?

C. When he was confronted by Samuel, what was his response?

D. *See verse 28.* What was the result of Saul's disobedience?

E. How did Saul's actions affect Samuel?

F. Do you feel others are affected by our obedience or disobedience to God? Why or why not?

3. *Read 1 Samuel 1; 2:1-11, 18-21.*

A. What are some natural reasons for Hannah to go back on the promise she made to give Samuel up to God?

B. *See chapter 2, verses 1-11.* From the previous chapter

and this passage, what do you know about Hannah's relationship with God?

C. *See chapter 2, verses 18-21.* What kind of mother was Hannah?

D. What was the result of Hannah's "relinquishment" (verses 20-21)?

Further Reflections: On a separate sheet of paper, list several things that you want more than anything else in the world. Now go back and analyze them. Are your desires for the eternal? The temporal? Self?

Remember: God is interested in more than our physical comfort or material needs although we trust Him for those things too. His ultimate purpose is for us to learn how to obey Him in all of life.

Catherine Marshall wrote:

> Self will turn the eyes on self
> and what self strongly wants;
> Faith turns the eyes on Christ
> to ask Him what He wants.

Self worries about results.
Faith worries only about obedience—
    and leaves results to Jesus.

We all struggle with different "Isaacs" at different times in our lives. Our children are classic examples of this. We have them in our care and love them intensely. But they are God's, not ours.

The beauty of our walk with God is that *after* the cross there is the resurrection. *After* discipline comes peace and joy. *After* obedience comes blessing. Our God is not a miserly, harsh God. He loves us and knows what is best for us.

Martin Luther said, *"I have held many things in my hands and have lost them all. . . . But whatsoever I have placed in God's hands, that I still possess."*

IV

Knowing God

Discerning God's Voice

ॐ

Why Pray?

ॐ

The Comforter

ॐ

His Name Is Jesus

Discerning God's Voice

Today's Theme: Cleansing our minds and lives through meditation on God's Word.

Moments in Prayer: *"Lord, many voices call to us today. They clamor for our attention—begging to be heard and entertained. Help us to filter them out with Your Word so we can hear Your still, small voice and, in doing so, see our world through Your eyes. In Jesus' name, Amen."*

Scripture Reading: Read Psalm 51 meditatively. There are other Scriptures that we will be referring to, but the basic theme will come from this psalm.

Introductory Insights: Never before has the human mind been so invaded. The blessings of the media are a two-edged sword. While we are privileged with more information, with that information comes the burden of endless choices.

As radios, televisions, newspapers, magazines, billboards and even the messages on our cereal boxes fill our minds with information, we are tempted to become merely *consumers*, targeted to fill someone's profit margin or political agenda.

We are neatly packaged and labeled as a "yuppie," "tradition-alist," "evangelical," "republican," "democrat," "working mother," "nonworking mother" or "single parent." Once labeled, the media grabs on to us with more specific claims, telling us what we "need" to fit into our particular stratum of society.

How can I—God's child—discern God's voice through all the competing noise? What is God saying to me individually? Psalm 51, especially verses 10-12, will give us some insight into answering these questions.

Digging into the Details:

1. *"Create in me a clean heart, O God..."*—Acknowledgement of sin, need for cleansing.

A. "Sin" is being edited out of our vocabulary today and is being replaced by words like "sickness" or "weakness." *Read Isaiah 53:6; Psalm 51:5; Romans 3:23.* What do these Scriptures say about sin?

B. *Read Isaiah 53:4-5; Psalm 51:1-3; 1 John 1:7-9.* What is the solution for sin?

2. *"... and renew a right spirit within me"*—Recognition of our sinful nature, a continual warfare.

A. There is an enemy of our souls. He attacks us by appealing to our sin nature, our base desires and personal areas where we are most vulnerable. *Read 2 Corinthians 10:3-5; Ephesians 6:10-13; Hebrews 12:1-2.* Write down ways we can combat these attacks.

B. *Read Romans 12:1-2.* What does God promise to renew, and what does He require for this to take place?

C. *Read Psalm 19:12-14.* What do you believe are "secret faults" (see verse 12)? How would they differ from "presumptuous sins" (see verse 13)?

D. How can we be protected from both kinds of sin (see Psalm 19:7-11)?

3. *"Restore unto me the joy . . ."*—Recognition of a powerful God, mighty on our behalf.

A. *Read Psalm 77.* In verses 1-6, what was the psalmist's frame of mind?

B. In verses 7-9, what type of questions is he asking?

C. *Read verses 10-12.* Notice the change in thought patterns, resulting in verses 13-20. What do you believe caused the change?

D. *Read Philippians 4:6-9.* From this Scripture, what specific thought-disciplines can help restore joy in our lives?

Further Reflections: Proverbs 4:26 says, *"Ponder the path of thy feet, and let all thy ways be established"* (KJV). There are times for *pondering.* Mothers ponder over their children, as Mary the mother of Jesus did, prayerfully considering, "Is this God's intervention? Is this the right way?"

There are times we must ponder our own paths. Considering the constant "input" we receive from our world, it's good to take an occasional personal inventory and ask ourselves some hard questions: What is the main thrust of my life? Who am I influencing for righteousness? What "secret faults" and "presumptuous sins" plague me? Do I see God as big as He really is? Is my life overflowing with praise and worship to Him—regardless of my circumstances? Do I remember to thank God for the good things He has done in the past and trust Him for the future?

Why Pray?

God calls us to come into His presence.

Today's Theme: Developing a prayer life that will increase our capacity to know God.

Moments in Prayer: *"Lord, how glibly we promise to pray, but how easily we allow the 'tyranny of the urgent' to rule our lives. And yet in these pressure-filled days we long to see Your face, to hear Your voice more than ever. We pray that we will become disciplined to seek after You. Amen."*

Scripture Reading: Song of Solomon 2:8-15; Isaiah 40:28-31; Luke 11:1-3.

Introductory Insights: Why do we pray? Just because it's a good thing to do? Because we're afraid? Because we have needs? Or is it an opportunity to touch the divine—to become a friend of God? What a privilege to communicate with the Creator of the universe—a personal God who is concerned with the intimate details of our lives!

Catherine Marshall wrote, "God wants a relationship with us. A two-way relationship—asking and receiving. The reason many of us retreat into vague generalities when we pray is not because we think too highly of God, but because we think too little."

Catch a glimpse of the heart of God as He calls to us, "Rise up, my love, my fair one, and come away! . . . Let me see your countenance, let me hear your voice" (Song of Solomon 2:13-14). Remember that He is "able to do exceedingly abundantly above all that we ask or think . . ." (Ephesians 3:20). "Delight yourself also in the Lord, and He shall give you the desires of your heart" (Psalm 37:4).

Too often we rush into God's presence with our "grocery list" of needs that we rattle upward and then we rush off again. We pause later perhaps and wonder why God hasn't answered our prayers. Maybe He has. Maybe we're not listening. Just as for a growing marriage we must sharpen our communication skills, so we must develop the art—the discipline—of prayer if we are to grow closer to God.

Digging into the Details:

1. The Discipline of a Place. *Read Song of Solomon 2:8-15.*

A. Compare this love story to our relationship with God.

B. What are some "little foxes" that can spoil our relationship with God?

C. *See Mark 6:31,46; 14:32-42.* List the places where Jesus went to pray.

D. Why must we also "come away" to pray?

2. The Discipline of Praise. *Read Psalm 34:1-4; Psalm 100; and Philippians 4:6-7.*

A. Psalm 100:4 says to "enter into His gates with thanksgiving and . . . praise." Why is this important?

B. *See Psalm 34:1-4.* The first verse begins with an action and the fourth verse contains a consequence. Describe them.

C. *See Philippians 4:6-7.* Again, describe the consequences of thanksgiving in prayer.

3. The Discipline of Waiting. *Read Isaiah 40:28-31.*

   A. What do you think it means to wait on God?

   B. What benefits could be experienced by listening to God *before* we begin our petitions?

   C. What are the consequences of waiting on God (verse 31)?

4. The Discipline of Asking. *Read Luke 11:1-13.*

   A. What kinds of things are we to ask for?

   B. *See Matthew 18:10-20.* Describe what this passage says about united prayer.

Further Reflections: Jesus often referred to fasting when discussing prayer. Andrew Murray wrote, "Prayer needs fasting for its full growth. Prayer is the one hand with which we grasp the invisible; fasting, the other with which we let loose and cast away the visible. . . . The first thought suggested by Jesus' words in regards to fasting and prayer is that it is only in a life of moderation and temperance and self-denial that there will be the heart or strength to pray much."*

Here are some additional references to fasting that you may wish to read: Psalm 35:13; Matthew 6:17; 17:21; and 1 Corinthians 7:5.

Points to Ponder: Have you noticed a pattern for prayer?

- ❧ First, come away into His presence (deliberate intention, shutting out distractions).

- ❧ Second, enter His presence with praise and thanksgiving (with our focus on an almighty God, we see *Him*, not the problems).

- ❧ Third, wait and listen (to discern *how* to pray).

- ❧ Fourth, ask—because we're His much-loved children.

The Difference

I got up early one morning
    and rushed right into the day;
I had so much to accomplish,
    that I didn't have time to pray.

Problems just tumbled about me,
    and heavier came each task.

---

* Andrew Murray, *With Christ in the School of Prayer* (Springdale, PA: Whitaker House, 1981).

"Why doesn't God help me?" I
   wondered.
   He answered, "You didn't ask."

I wanted to see joy and beauty,
   but the day toiled on, gray and bleak;
I wondered why God didn't show me.
   He said, "But you didn't seek."

I tried to come into God's presence;
   I used all my keys at the lock.
God gently and lovingly chided,
   "My child, you didn't knock."

I woke up early this morning,
   and paused before entering the day,
I had so much to accomplish
   that I had to take time to pray.
                          —*Author unknown*

The Comforter

Today's Theme: Learning to receive and give comfort.

Moments in Prayer: *"Lord, You promised that You would not leave us 'comfortless'—that You would come to us. We pray that we may comprehend what that means and, in turn, comfort others as we have been comforted. Amen."*

Scripture Reading: John 14:16-26; 2 Corinthians 1:3-7. (Other Scriptures are listed below.)

Introductory Insights: Comfort . . . it's a *comfortable* word. It brings to mind a mug of steaming hot tea in front of a fireplace . . . dear, old friends with whom you can laugh and talk easily . . . sunshine after rain . . . freedom from fear or pain . . . relief . . . hope . . . a hug . . . a touch of kindness when you need it most . . . the presence of one whom you love very much . . . a sudden realization that life *is* good after all. Jesus promised that He would not leave us comfortless, that He would come to us (John 14:18).

When Jesus returned to heaven, He sent the Holy Spirit— the Comforter—to be with us. "Comforter" is taken from the Greek *parakletos* which means "one called to the side of another for help or counsel."

96

Have you ever seen a child who was angry and hurt, yet refused to be comforted? We can be like that at times. The drive to be independent, to make it on our own, is strong. And yet the world can be scary at times. Terrible things can happen, or just crummy, disappointing things. We fail, we sin. And that's when we realize more than ever that we need the Comforter.

We are going to look at nine different ways that God comforts us.

Digging into the Details: *God offers comfort through . . .*
1. *The Word.* Read Romans 15:4; John 14–16.

    A. In what ways do these verses offer comfort?

    B. Was there a time in your life when you received comfort from Scripture? If so, describe this time.

2. *Forgiveness.* Read Genesis 50:15-21; Isaiah 40:1-2; 2 Samuel 12:13-24.

    A. From reading the passage about Joseph (Genesis 50), why do you think his brothers needed comfort?

B. In your opinion, how can pardon from iniquity bring comfort (Isaiah 40:1-2)?

C. Read the passages about David's sin, then describe what we can learn from this tragedy (2 Samuel 12:15-24; Psalm 51:10-13).

3. *Preaching*. Read 1 Corinthians 14:3,31.

A. Preaching God's Word is to edify and exhort the believer. Describe what this means and how it should bring comfort.

B. Describe a time when you received comfort through the preaching of the Word.

4. *Seeing His hand in the miraculous*. Read Acts 20:7-12.

A. Describe why you think the believers in Troas were comforted because of this miracle.

B. Can you describe a miracle that has happened in your life—something that "couldn't-be-just-coincidence"? Of course we must believe without seeing, but what makes a miracle special?

5. *The love and compassion of others.* Read Ruth 2:1-14; Colossians 4:7-9.

A. How did Boaz offer comfort to Ruth? Why do you think Ruth was in special need of comfort?

B. How was Paul offering comfort to the Colossians (Colossians 4:7-9)?

C. From these two examples, what can we learn about receiving comfort from others?

D. Describe a time when you have been comforted by someone.

6. *The blessed hope.* Read 1 Thessalonians 4:13-18; 5:1-11; Revelation 21:1-7.

A. Describe in your own words this wonderful mystery (1 Thessalonians 4:13-18).

B. Why does this thought comfort you?

C. List several things from Revelation 21:1-7 that give the believer hope and comfort.

7. *Physical restoration and refreshment.* Read Genesis 50:21; Job 42:11; 1 Kings 19:1-8.

A. The passages in Genesis and 1 Kings describe people being comforted through what physical means?

B. In what practical ways was Job comforted?

C. How can we apply this very common but essential principle in order to bring comfort to others?

8. *Our own will.* Read Psalm 119:52; Philippians 4:6-9.

A. How did the psalmist bring comfort to himself?

B. Do you believe it is possible to refuse God's comfort? How?

C. How can we by our own choice choose to accept God's presence (Philippians 4:6-9)?

9. *When we comfort others.* Read 2 Corinthians 9:7-8; Mark 4:24-25; Luke 6:38.

A. What do these Scriptures say about the principle of giving?

B. Do you believe it's possible to receive comfort yourself by giving comfort to others? If you have experienced this personally, describe.

Further Reflections: A friend who was experiencing physical pain with an ailment described an unusual way she received comfort. She said, "I was having a very bad night, the pain worse than I'd ever had. I tried all the remedies—the prescription, warm milk, relaxing bath. Nothing worked. My husband was out of town so I was feeling very alone and was at the point of despair. Finally it occurred to me that many others also had pain. So I began to pray for everyone I knew who was in pain or in any other negative circumstances. I thanked God for the answers, for the wonderful ways He had provided in the past, and before I knew it I drifted into a sound sleep. I awoke the next morning, refreshed and grateful."

What keeps us from accepting God's comfort? Pride? Self-sufficiency? The desire to hang onto something just because we're used to it? Whatever it is, it isn't worth it. God freely offers His comfort to us through His presence.

Points to Ponder:

❧ Am I refusing God's comfort? Why?

❧ How can I offer comfort to someone today?

His Name Is Jesus

Today's Theme: Examining the different names of our Lord and what they mean to us.

"... And His Name will be called Wonderful, Counselor, Mighty God, Everlasting Father, Prince of Peace ..." (Isaiah 9:6).

Moments in Prayer: *"Lord, we pray that we will be able to comprehend and accept the love, forgiveness, healing, hope and provision that there is in the magnificent, strong name of Jesus. Amen."*

Scripture Reading: Genesis 15:1,7; Genesis 17. (Other Scriptures are listed in the exercises below.)

Introductory Insights: If you have a child, you undoubtedly remember the delicate process of naming him or her. Some parents name their children after relatives or special friends. Other parents choose names just because they like the sound. And some parents choose names for their meanings. At any rate, your name is very important! As you grow and mature, you become identified with your name—it's your calling card. *Who you are is represented by your name.* That's why uncomplimentary nicknames can hurt—they strike at the essence of who we are.

There are many names that describe God. When God presented His credentials to Abram (Genesis 15 and 17), He told him who He was, what He would do for him and his descendants and what He required of them.

When we come to God—regardless of our need—He will reveal an aspect of His character to us. He meets us where we are. James 4:8 says, "Draw near to God and He will draw near to you."

This is a study of some of the different Hebrew names ascribed to God which show His character and nature. As you go through this exercise, prayerfully meditate on each description and ask the Lord to increase your understanding and faith in His name.

Digging into the Details:
1. *Immanuel*—"God With us." *Read Isaiah 7:14 and Matthew 1:23.* "Jesus" is the Greek form of the Hebrew Jehosua (rendered Joshua), meaning "Savior" or "God Who Is Salvation."

How have you personally experienced "Immanuel" (God's presence in your life)?

2. *El-Olam*—"The Eternally Existent One." *Read Hebrews 1:10-12; 13:8; and Psalm 90.*

A. What do these Scriptures say about man's nature versus God's?

B. Describe your personal feelings about these verses.

3. *El-Shaddai*—"God Almighty, Giver of Strength." *Read Psalm 18:31-32; 91:1-2; Isaiah 40:29-31; 41:10.*

A. What do these verses say about God's strength?

B. From these Scriptures describe how we can learn to apply God's strength to our own lives.

4. *Jehovah*—"The Self-Existent One." This is God's redemptive name which can also be rendered as "Lord" or "Adonai." *Read Exodus 6:1-8 and Isaiah 12:1-3.*

From these passages, describe what is involved in redemption.

5. *Jehovah-Jireh*—"The Lord Will Provide." *Read Genesis 22:1-14 and Matthew 6:8.*

    A. What did Abraham experience on Mount Moriah?

    B. How is the passage in Matthew similar to the one in Genesis 22? What can you apply from these teachings to your own situation?

6. *Jehovah-Shalom*—"The Lord Our Peace" (also signifies wholeness). *Read Isaiah 26:3; 57:15-21; John 14:27; and Philippians 4:6-9.*
From reading these Scriptures, what are some conditions we must meet to experience God's peace?

7. *Jehovah-Ropheka*—"The Lord Your (Personal) Physician." *Read Psalm 41:4; 103:1-3; 147:3; Jeremiah 3:22; and Malachi 4:2.*
Describe some of the ways the Lord heals us.

8. *Jehovah-Shammah*—"The Lord Is There." This name is a figurative reference to Jerusalem during the millennial reign of Christ. *Read Revelation 21:3-7.*

What does this intimate portrait of a caring, involved, "in-charge" Lord mean to you? Why?

9. *Jehovah-Raah*—"The Lord My Shepherd." *Read Psalm 23; Isaiah 40:11; and John 10.*

Go through these Scriptures and compare the example of "sheep and shepherd" to our relationship with the Lord.

10. *Jehovah-Tsidkeenu*—"The Lord Our Righteousness." *Read Jeremiah 23:6; Romans 9:30-33; Galatians 6:5; and Ephesians 2:8-10.*

A. What are some ways that we attempt righteousness through human efforts?

B. Why is it impossible to become righteous through our own efforts?

Further Reflections:

1. Take a moment to reflect on the events of the past year in your personal life. Now look again at the different meanings of our Lord's name. Write down or share with others an aspect of God's nature that has been especially meaningful to you and describe why.

2. In examining your life today, what aspect of God's nature or character do you need for the unique challenges in your life at this time? Remember, "The name of the Lord is a strong tower; the righteous run to it and are safe" (Proverbs 18:10).

V

Developing Inner Beauty

How to Be Clothed
in Strength

❧

Beauty that Lasts

❧

Your Intrinsic Value

❧

Growing Up

❧

When Life Is Unfair

How to Be Clothed in Strength

Waiting on God renews our strength.

Today's Theme: Developing spiritual strength through waiting on God.

Moments in Prayer: *"Lord, show me how to wait on You to renew my strength. Amen."*

Scripture Reading: Isaiah 40:28-31; 30:15-18; 2 Corinthians 4:7-18; 12:7-10; Romans 4:3-6; Psalm 86:15-16.

Digging into the Details:
1. *Understanding God's Nature.*

   A. Reread Isaiah 40:28-31, Psalm 86:15-16. These passages tell of the character of God. List some key words that describe God's nature.

   B. What does it mean to "wait on the Lord"?

   C. Describe why waiting on God is easier when you

understand who God is and His intentions toward you, His child.

2. *Understanding Our Humanity.*

A. In Isaiah 6:1-8, Isaiah had a vision of the Lord. His reaction was an overwhelming sense of his own humanity (see verse 5). What was Isaiah's response to God (verse 8)?

B. Reread 2 Corinthians 4:7-18. What are some strong reminders of our humanity?

3. *Dealing with Weaknesses.*

Paul gives a powerful insight into tapping the secret of spiritual strength in 2 Corinthians 12:7-10. (Reread these verses.) A better word for "thorn" is a "stake" in the flesh, such as a stake used in a crucifixion.

There seems to be no doubt that Paul had a very painful, irritating physical condition. He asked the Lord to deliver him *thrice*, a Hebrew figure of speech meaning ceaselessly or over and over again. His prayer seemed to be unanswered. The message finally came from God: "My grace is sufficient for you, for My strength is made perfect in weakness" (verse 9). *In weakness is strength* (2 Corinthians 12:10)!

A. Do you have a "thorn in the flesh"? What should be your attitude toward it (Romans 5:3-6)?

B. Realizing our weaknesses does not mean low self-esteem, lack of confidence or depression. Reread 2 Corinthians 12:7-10. What positive mental attitudes do you see reflected in this passage?

C. Is it possible to become "strong" (physically, materially, intellectually) and in the process become spiritually "weak"? If so, how can you enjoy success and still avoid the pitfalls (Jeremiah 9:23-24)?

Strength is something that becomes used up, depleted. It needs to be renewed. Have you been getting insights on how to "wait on God" for renewed strength?

Often things come into our lives that we see as interruptions. Perhaps it's an unplanned pregnancy, surgery or an illness. This "interruption" *can be* the catalyst to cause us to wait upon God, rejoicing in Him always.

Wait on God and watch for results. He will renew your strength, and you will ". . . mount up with wings like eagles . . . run and not be weary . . . walk and not faint" (Isaiah 40:31).

Further Reflections:

1. Proverbs 31:25 says the virtuous woman is clothed in "strength and honor" and "she shall rejoice in time to come." Another paraphrase says she is "... not afraid of old age." What do you think is the secret of growing older "covered with strength"?

2. How important is it to "rejoice in the Lord always" (Philippians 4:4)?

3. Now go back to the list of things that impressed you about the original passages in the "Reading" section. Find key words and thoughts in those verses. If you have a cross-reference Bible, there will be other references in the margin that will give you additional insights.

If you have a concordance, look up other passages with key words that refer to the same subject. Most importantly, spend time meditating on these passages.

Beauty that Lasts

Today's Theme: Developing inner qualities that reflect the beauty of our Lord.

Moments in Prayer: "Lord, we pray that as we spend time looking into the mirror of Your Word, we will have the willingness and courage to be changed to reflect Your glory. Amen."

Scripture Reading: Read 1 Peter 2; 3:1-7; 2 Corinthians 2:14-17; 3–5.

Introductory Insights: Everybody wants to look good these days. It's important, people say, to have the right image. It enhances our business, "ministry" and self-esteem.

"Looking good" is an enormous industry. Millions of dollars are spent on cosmetics, face-lifts, hair treatments, spas and any other beauty treatment possible.

One can't help but compare this to how much time is spent on developing the intellect and godly character traits that last. While it is true that we should do the best we can with what we have physically, even the most phenomenal magic wrinkle-removal formulas won't stop aging. Eventually, outward beauty will fade and we will all look old.

The Bible, however, refers to "incorruptible" beauty (1 Peter 3:4). You've seen it in certain women—perhaps in their 70s and 80s—who possess that elusive, quiet beauty and deep strength, coupled with a good sense of humor, approachability and a certain gracefulness toward life. They have a deep, unshakable trust and confidence in God. What is their secret?

Digging into the Details:
1. *Read 2 Corinthians 2:14-17.*

    A. What mental pictures come to your mind as you read these verses?

    B. What makes us fragrant with Christ's presence (verses 14-15)?

    C. Because of erroneous teaching, too many women equate spirituality with timidity, uncertainty and powerlessness. How do the above verses and also Romans 8:15-17 refute this?

2. *Read 2 Corinthians 3:1-5; 1 Peter 2:1-10.*

A. Who—or what—is the "cornerstone" or "bottom line" of your life? How is this evidenced in your life?

B. Why is it impossible to remain neutral about Jesus Christ?

C. What are the consequences of unbelief (see 1 Peter 2:8; 2 Corinthians 2:16)?

3. *Read 2 Corinthians 4–5.*

A. List some things in your world that have temporal value.

B. List some things in your world that you feel have eternal value.

C. How can you order your life so that your temporal world is in proper perspective to your spiritual world?

Further Reflections: Many women have read 1 Peter 3:1-5 and have taken the passage exclusively without reading the rest of Scripture, therefore missing the spirit of the law.

The epistle is written to teach believers how to live before an unbelieving world. This particular portion of the epistle is a beautiful teaching on how to live the Gospel before an unbelieving husband.

There is much confusion on the matter of submission and roles in marriage. Lloyd Ogilvie says, "Love is at the root of the biblical understanding of submission. The Scripture tells us that Jesus submitted to the Father because of His deep love for Him and that He submitted to the cross because of His deep love for us.

"To submit is not to be inferior. To the contrary, Jesus was equal with God, but He emptied Himself in submission by becoming a servant.

"A Christian marriage is predicated upon the same principles. A woman is not inferior or superior to a man in marriage. In Christ 'there is neither male nor female; for you are all one in Christ Jesus' (Galatians 3:28) . . . mutual submission within the body of Christ is an even higher principle. It is the key to Christian marriage."

The deep kind of beauty, "the hidden person of the heart with the incorruptible ornament of a gentle and quiet spirit," reflects a person who is not motivated by fear. "Perfect love casts out fear" (1 John 4:18).

1. It has been said that the five greatest enemies of peace are avarice, ambition, envy, anger and pride. Do you believe it is possible to structure circumstances around you so that you will develop a peaceful and quiet spirit? Why or why not?

2. *Read Isaiah 26:3; Psalm 119:165; John 14:27; Romans 8:6.* What do these verses say about developing an *attitude* of peace?

Points to Ponder: Ask yourself the following three questions:

❧ Do I know who I am in God?

❧ Do I understand my purpose in life?

❧ Am I engaged in fulfilling that purpose?

Your Intrinsic Value

God has intimate care for each of us.

Today's Theme: Self-worth—comprehending our Father's love.

Moments in Prayer: *"Thank You, God, for all of Your wonderful creation—including* me. *Thank You for making me an individual with unique opportunities. Show me, through Your Word, my intrinsic value to You. Amen."*

Scripture Reading: Psalm 139; Ephesians 2:1-10; Matthew 6:25-34; Hebrews 12:1-2; Romans 8:1; 9:20-23; Hebrews 4:14-16; Psalm 103; Isaiah 53:4-6.

Digging into the Details:

1. The following passages show the intimate care that God has for us. Look up each reference and write down evidence of our heavenly Father's love for us.

   A. Psalm 139:

B. Ephesians 2:1-10:

C. Matthew 6:25-34:

2. *Read Hebrews 12:1-2.*

A. Poor self-esteem is a "weight" that hinders our race. List some ways a poor self-image affects you, your family, husband, relatives, friends, work, witness for Christ.

B. How does a *proper* understanding of who we are in Christ turn each of the above relationships into a constructive force?

3. *Read Romans 8:1; 9:20-23.*

We often have a tendency to tear ourselves down. Why is it wrong for us to deny our self-worth?

4. Perhaps your image of a loving God is distorted due to early hurts or wrong teaching in your life. Look up and read the following passages meditatively. Then "rewrite" the verses with your own specific needs, names, blessings, etc. (For example, Hebrews 4:14-15: "I, Susan, have a great High Priest who cares about me so much that He is touched by my feelings of inadequacy, of hurt. But He invites me to come boldly into His presence where He will give me all the help I need. . . .")

A. Hebrews 4:14-16:

B. Psalm 103:

C. Isaiah 53:4-6:

Meditate on Scripture that ministers to your deepest needs, building you up. You may want to write these verses on cards and keep them handy in places like your purse, on the refrigerator or in your car. Passages such as Philippians 4:7-8 and Ephesians 6 are good places to start.

Further Reflections: Read Matthew 7:24-27 (parable of the wise man building his house on the rock).

Too many of us build our "houses" on things other than the Rock, Christ Jesus. As wonderful as family, marriage or meaningful work are, they will not last. We cannot put our hope for self-esteem in temporal things such as our appearance, good works, monetary value or "success." All of these will eventually run out, and we will be left standing with the questions: "Where does my 'wholeness' lie? What gives me security?"

Colossians 1:27 says, "Christ in you" is your only "hope of glory," and 2 Corinthians 4:7 reminds us, "But we have this treasure in earthen vessels. . . ."

There is a beautiful description in John 13 of Jesus washing the disciples' feet. Jesus does this very mundane, necessary, dirty job with complete grace and dignity. The key is in verse 3: "Jesus, knowing that the Father had given all things into His hands, and that He had come from God and was going to God, rose. . . ." Jesus knew the Father, and He knew Himself.

The more we know God and understand His purpose for our lives, the more directed and fulfilled our lives become. We are then able to have an attitude of *self-forgetfulness* rather than *self-consciousness* as we respond to the needs in our world.

Points to Ponder:

🕱 Why do we lose sight of the wonderful "treasure" (God's presence) that we have within us?

🕱 Read Romans 12:1-2. How can we exercise "transformed" thinking to counteract the constant barrage from our world on what makes us valuable?

Growing Up

Today's Theme: Christian maturity.

Moments in Prayer: "Thank You, God, that You do not forsake the work of Your hands. Show me how I can grow in character and maturity. In Jesus' name, Amen."

Scripture Reading: Ephesians 2:1-10, 4–5; 2 Corinthians 6:11-13; 7:1-3; Philippians 3; 1 Corinthians 1:10-31; Galatians 2–5.

Introductory Insights: In our youth-oriented culture it's hard to get enthusiastic about *maturity*. We have visions of pension plans, gray hair, wrinkles—all those inevitable things we want to postpone.

But God urges us to "grow up in all things into Him" (Ephesians 4:15). He knows spiritual maturity is a wonderful, freeing development. Our chronological age is not the criterion; we can be 20 and developing maturity or we can be 60 and be spiritually immature. It's a matter of application of God's truth in our lives.

Digging into the Details: Steps to Maturity
1. *Read Ephesians 2:1-10.*

A. What does this passage tell about the basic nature of man *before Christ*?

B. What is the "gift" of God (verse 8), and what difference does it make when we accept it?

2. *Read Ephesians 4–5.*

A. How is it possible to have unity and still have diversity?

B. What verses in these passages show us how to love others when it seems impossible?

3. *Read 2 Corinthians 6:11-13; 7:1-3.*

A. What do these verses say about being open and honest with one another?

B. In your opinion, how does being open with each other help us move toward maturity?

Hindrances to Maturity
1. Read Philippians 3, concentrating especially on verses 12-16.
How can our past successes or failures hinder maturity?

2. Read 1 Corinthians 1:10-31.

A. What was causing the Corinthians to become sidetracked in their Christian growth?

B. How can we avoid this trap today?

3. Read Galatians 2–5.

A. Why is earning our salvation or trying to win approval through works an impossible task?

B. In what ways do you see Christians today being caught up in legalism?

C. How does this hinder maturity?

Further Reflections: Maturity comes when someone is able to get past his or her own needs and expectations to realize these facts:

1. I know that God loves me with an everlasting love (Romans 8).

2. He divinely orders my steps and circumstances (Psalm 1).

3. Regardless of others' responses, attitudes and actions, *I will obey God* (Philippians 3:13-14).

4. I will open up to and love in His name those He brings into my life (1 Corinthians 13).

Philippians 4:19 says, "My God shall supply all your need according to His riches in glory by Christ Jesus."

Who is your source for emotional fulfillment? As special as it is to have a loving husband, children and friends, only God can meet all your deepest needs. Only *He* is perfect; only *He* never fails.

The amazing thing is that when we realize we are loved with His agape love, then we are able to love others with His agape love. That's real maturity.

When Life Is Unfair

God can handle our questions.

Today's Theme: How to respond when affected by disappointment and/or trials.

Moments in Prayer: *"Lord, it's easy to praise You when things go well. But there are times when hard things happen that we just do not understand. You said that You would never leave us or forsake us. Help us to trust even when—especially when—we do not have the answers. Amen."*

Scripture Reading: The entire Book of Job. (You may read just chapters 1–4, 8; 12; 15; 18–19; 22–23; 27; 32–34; 38–42.)

Introductory Insights: Life's full of injustices. If we look, they're all around us. A mother loses her only child. An infertile couple with empty arms reads in the paper of parents abusing (even murdering) their own children. A beautiful teenaged girl is paralyzed in a car accident then, shortly after, loses her mother to cancer. *Why,* we wonder. It doesn't make sense. The human suffering seems beyond comprehension.

We are oriented to think *cause and effect*, or *actions equal consequences.* We train our children that way when we reward good behavior and punish the bad. We teach and believe that what we sow, we reap. And for much of life, that is true. Yet there are those times when the unexplainable and unthinkable happen. For every David, there is a Job. For every Peter delivered out of prison, there is a John the Baptist who doesn't make it.

Job was a man who lived during the pre-law era, shortly before the Exodus. The first, second and last chapters of Job are written in a simple narrative and the rest—conversations between Job and his friends and God—in poetic form. Tradition says that Moses authored the book.

Job, a righteous man, suffers the loss of his children, possessions, and health. God withdraws His protection from Job, and Satan is permitted to inflict harm as he tries to prove that Job is righteous only because God has greatly blessed him. The Book of Job is a treatise on why the righteous suffer. It also describes the reactions of those close to him during his suffering. We see Job's anger and depression during this process and how God speaks to Job and ultimately restores him.

Digging into the Details:
1. "The Calamities." *Read Job 1–2.*

A. From the information available, what kind of family do you think Job had? (1:4-5; 18)

B. What kind of father was Job? (1:1,5)

C. According to this passage of Scripture, why did these calamities happen?

D. What limits did God put on Satan? (2:6)

E. Was Job's wife right to blame God? Why or why not?

2. "The Response to Job's Suffering by His Friends." *Write a synopsis of each friend's view of Job's suffering* (see Scripture references below).

A. Eliphaz: He argued from the standpoint of *human experience* (chapters 4–5, 15, and 22).

B. Bildad: He argued from *human tradition* (chapters 8; 18; and 25).

C. Zophar: He argued from *human merit* (chapters 11 and 20).

D. Why do you think it is a common human response to want to have a solution or reason for everything?

3. Job's Reaction." *Read chapters 9, 12–13, and 19.*

A. Do you believe that Job's agony was increased by his friends' counsel (9:32-35; 6:6; 12–13)?

B. From reading chapter 23, what do you think is Job's concept of God? What does he believe God is doing in his life?

C. From reading chapter 27:2-6, what would you say is Job's stance of faith?

D. Read chapters 38–39. What kind of things does God tell Job?

Further Reflections: *Read chapter 42.* Here we see Job restored in a beautiful way. He responds to God in humility and faith. God, angry at Job's friends for misrepresenting Him, instructs them to offer a sacrifice. Verse 10 says, "The Lord restored Job's losses when he prayed for his friends. Indeed the Lord gave Job twice as much as he had before." This is a powerful picture of grace and forgiveness. Many of us who have experienced losses can remember unfeeling or hurtful things people said to us at the time. They meant well, but when we are hurting, we are particularly vulnerable to comments. The lesson we can learn here is that we must forgive and pray for those who have hurt us in order that we may have complete healing and get on with our lives.

When a major loss happens, we often recoil with the "whys." God can handle our questions while He patiently loves us through the process. The good news to remember is that Jesus said, "In the world you will have tribulation; but be of good cheer, I have overcome the world" (John 16:33).

Points to Ponder: What can we learn—if anything—from pain and loss?

  ❧ Total trust and reliance on God.

  ❧ Patience—waiting to see the entire picture.

  ❧ How to comfort others in their pain.

I walked a mile with Pleasure,
She chattered all the way;
But left me none the wiser
As she went on her way.
I walked a mile with Sorrow;
And not a word said she,
But O, the things I learned
When Sorrow walked with me.

—Robert Browning Hamilton

VI

Fruit: Evidence of a Relationship

Gifts from the Heart

❧

The Garment of Praise

❧

Convinced of God's Goodness

❧

Water for Thirsty People

❧

The Key to Contentment

Gifts from the Heart

Today's Theme: Accepting the challenge through Scripture to give of our *essence*, the most central part of our lives.

Moments in Prayer: "Lord, teach us what it means to give of ourselves without hesitation or reserve—purely for the love of You. Amen."

Scripture Reading: Mark 12:41-44; 2 Corinthians 8–9; Luke 6:38; John 3:16-23.

Introductory Insights: Although our culture is different from biblical times, certain basics have not changed. God's work still requires our resources and our time.

Have you ever heard someone pray over an offering, *". . . bless those who give and those who cannot give . . ."*? I wonder what the poor widow who gave all she had (just a fraction of a cent) would think of such a prayer—or the boy who gave all he had—five small loaves and two fish. The point is, everyone has *something* he or she can give.

In 2 Kings 4, there is the story of a woman in dire need. Her husband had been in Elisha's school of the prophets and had died, leaving her and her two sons heavily in debt. The creditors were about to take her sons into slavery. When she went to

Elisha in desperation, he asked her, "What do you have in your house?" Her reply: "Nothing . . . *except a jar of oil.*"

How typical! God asks us, "What do you have?" And we say, "Nothing." Then we begin to think: *except I do have a home . . . a car . . . a telephone. I have some time on Saturday to visit a rest home. I can write someone an encouraging note. I can smile. I can pray. I can live without that new dress and give the money to missions.*

Wealth and talent are not prerequisites to the dynamic of giving as we will see in the following Scripture lessons.

Digging into the Details:
1. *Read Mark 12:41-44.*

A. From these four verses, what facts do you know about the woman?

B. What do you learn about the other people putting money into the treasury?

C. *Reread verses 43-44.* According to Jesus, why was the widow's gift more meaningful?

2. *Read 2 Corinthians 8–9.*

A. *Reread 2 Corinthians 8:1-5.* Describe in your own words the giving of the Macedonian churches.

B. *Read 2 Corinthians 8:6-15.* Why does Paul endorse "giving" to the Corinthian church?

C. *Read 2 Corinthians 9:5-11 and Luke 6:38.* What do these verses say about the best way to give?

3. *Read 1 John 3:16-23.* How will a sincere love for God become obvious?

Further Reflections: There are subtleties in the mystery of giving. At times we can give (perhaps unconsciously) out of selfish motivation. We want to be liked, accepted. We want to impress.

James 1:27 says that true religion is to minister to widows and orphans and to the "least of these" that Jesus referred to in Matthew 25:40. Perhaps true giving is giving to people who cannot pay you back.

I have noticed that often when we skim off the surplus, the "cream," and give that it does not seem nearly as memorable as the gift that comes right out of the heart—out of the need, out of the emptiness or pain.

The gift that means the most costs more: the expensive perfume that Mary used to anoint Jesus, the widow's mite and, ultimately, the unspeakable Gift (2 Corinthians 9:15) to us of God's Son, Jesus.

Last year our children gave my husband and me a set of dishes for our anniversary. They pooled their summer earnings, emptied their toy banks and presented their gift with shining eyes and delight. We treasure those dishes not because of their inherent worth, but because they were given out of love and sacrifice.

Points to Ponder:

❧ Can you remember a gift that someone gave you that cost them a substantial amount, financially or emotionally? What does that gift mean to you, and why?

❧ Can you remember giving something—materially or otherwise—that cost you a great deal? What was your motivation? How did you feel about it?

❧ What are some ways that we can teach our children to give?

The Garment of Praise

Trust and worry are incompatible.

Today's Theme: Determining to live a life full of praise to God, regardless of circumstances.

Moments in Prayer: "Lord, I ask for Your perspective on life. Open my eyes to the beauty and benefits that are mine. Help me to always praise You. Amen."

Scripture Reading: Acts 16:16-34; Isaiah 61:3; Psalm 33–34; 63:1-8; 100; 107; 108:1-6.

Introductory Insights: The story of Paul and Silas in prison singing at midnight is a familiar one to many of us. Paul the apostle's life was characterized by praise. It seemed that whenever Paul got in prison, that was the time he really began to praise God! The whole epistle to the Philippians is full of this tremendous spirit of rejoicing in God and in 1 Thessalonians, Paul encourages us to "Rejoice always . . . in everything give thanks" (5:16,18).

My husband, Bill, and I visited the Mammertine prison in Rome where it is believed that Paul wrote these epistles. It's a small, cold, dungeon-like room with rock walls.

Paul's joy is especially graphic when we contrast the massive rubble of the once-great Roman civilization with the

Mammertine prison. Paul knew he had something eternal—
"Jesus Christ...the same yesterday, today, and forever"
(Hebrews 13:8).

Digging into the Details:
1. *Read Acts 16:16-34.*

    A. Why were Paul and Silas put into prison?

    B. How was it possible for them to be praising God at midnight in a dungeon (verse 24)?

    C. What effect did their witness have on those around them?

    D. What are some principles from Paul and Silas' experience that you can apply to your own life?

2. *Read Isaiah 61:3 (also see Psalm 34:1-6).*

A. What does it mean to "put on" a garment of praise?

B. What are some of the "prisons" that hold us?

C. How will putting on praise free us?

3. *Read Psalm 33; 34:1-3.*

A. What different ways of praising God does this passage describe?

B. From these verses, list some reasons for praising God.

C. How will praising God bring peace and joy?

In *The Christian's Secret of a Happy Life* (Zondervan, 1984), Hannah Whitall Smith notes: "There are two things which are more utterly incompatible than even oil and water, and these two are trust and worry. Would you call it trust if you should give something into the hands of a friend to tend to for you, and then should spend your nights and days in anxious thoughts and worry as to whether it would be rightly and successfully done? And can you call it trust, when you have given the saving and keeping of your soul into the hands of the Lord, if day after day, and night after night you are spending hours of anxious thought and questionings about the matter? When a believer really trusts anything, he ceases to worry about that thing which he has trusted."

Further Reflection: Read Psalm 63:1-8; 100; 107; 108:1-6 and any other psalm of praise that is special to you. "Pray" these psalms to God. Take note of all God's provisions—especially His grace and mercy.

Perhaps you say, "Well, I don't *feel* like praising God. Things aren't going so well now." Feelings have nothing to do with praising God. God is worthy to be praised—regardless of feelings or circumstances.

For a picture to be developed, the negative must be plunged into developing solution. When we "plunge" our "negatives" into the presence of God via praise, we are able in a fresh way to see God at work.

Take one or more of the psalms and sing them to the Lord in your private devotions, or while driving, doing chores or going for a walk. Remember the song "Count Your Blessings"? You may want to follow this example and make a conscious effort to sit down and actually write praises to God.

Points to Ponder:

🍃 How does living a life of praise affect my life?

🍃 How does an attitude of praise affect those around me?

Convinced of God's Goodness

Today's Theme: Cultivating a grateful attitude.

Moments in Prayer: *"Lord, how natural it is for us to expect only perfection, the best and the easy way. Give us a broader view of life so we can see Your magnificent provision in all things. Free us from petty 'wants' and give us a grateful spirit, even in adversity. Amen."*

Scripture Reading: Exodus 6:1-13; 16; Numbers 11; Deuteronomy 8.

Introductory Insights: We live in a culture that makes it hard to be grateful for the basics—food, shelter and clothing. We don't just want ice cream—we want Häagan-Dazs. We aren't satisfied with merely a glass of water—we want Perrier. Johnny doesn't just crave a bike—he wants a BMX. Sally doesn't need tennis shoes—she needs Nikes.

It makes one wonder what our response would be if a modern Moses were to appear and tell us he was taking us out of Egypt to the Promised Land: "Pack up; let's go."

Maybe this was the problem with the children of Israel. All through the Exodus they complained and griped as they trudged along. We read of God miraculously delivering them out of Egypt, the dramatic escape through the Red Sea, the cloud by day and the fire by night, the manna from heaven, and the water from a rock.

Yet they complained and cried to go back to Egypt. So what if they were in bondage there—the leeks and onions tasted great! They had developed gourmet taste buds. They couldn't see beyond their immediate physical cravings to the ultimate goal—the Promised Land.

Digging into the Details:
1. *Read Exodus 6.*

A. How does this passage show that God was working on behalf of Israel?

B. Describe some characteristics of God's nature that you see in this chapter.

C. How does this encourage you?

2. *Read Exodus 16; Numbers 11:1-23.*

A. What was the attitude of the Israelites at this point (Exodus 16)?

B. How did Moses and Aaron react to the complaints of the Israelites (Exodus 16:7-8; Numbers 11:10-15)?

C. Describe how God tested their faith through the provision of manna (Exodus 16:12-35).

D. What is the difference between complaining and grumbling and sharing honest emotions?

3. *Read Deuteronomy 8.*

A. List several things the children of Israel learned about their relationship to God during their wilderness years.

B. What were the Israelites to remember after they were established in the Promised Land (verses 10-20)?

C. In what ways can we relate to this chapter practically and spiritually?

Further Reflections: The children of Israel began to take manna for granted. It was, after all, predictable, plentiful and nutritious. But can't you see the kids (and dads) roll their eyes at lunch and say, "This—*again?*"

It's easy for us to take common "miracles" for granted: health, food, a new day, God's creation, family and friends. We even complain about these at times.

One of my friends who is studying nursing said to me, "As I learn about the intricacies of the human body, I am more amazed at what goes right than at what goes wrong!"

We become ungrateful when we focus on the negative rather than the positive. We gaze longingly at the other side of the fence, unaware of the green beneath our own feet. It's like the boy lecturing his fussy little brother who wanted a double-scoop ice-cream cone rather than a single: "Andy, be thankful for what you get!"

Take time to meditate on these *Scriptures of Gratitude*: Psalm 100; 103; 2 Corinthians 9:6-15; Philippians 4:4-13; Colossians 3:15-17; and 1 Thessalonians 5:18.

We develop a grateful spirit when we are fully convinced of God's intimate and loving care of us, *regardless of the present circumstances.*

Points to Ponder:

❧ Sit down with your family (perhaps at a meal) and share ways you can develop grateful attitudes.

❧ Discuss a recent setback or adversity and analyze how you can give thanks *in it*.

❧ Read Jesus' commandment in Matthew 25:31-46 to visit the "least of these." How can obeying this commandment help you develop a grateful attitude?

❧ Share with others (especially your children) answers to prayer and miraculous provisions of God in years gone by. Remind one another of God's goodness as you mention past blessings.

John Greenleaf Whittier wrote:

> I know not where the fronded islands
>   lift their palms in prayer.
> I only know I cannot drift
>   beyond His love and care.

> —from *The Eternal Goodness*

Water for Thirsty People

Meet people at their point of need.

Today's Theme: Making good use of the opportunities you are given to tell others about Christ.

Moments in Prayer: *"Lord, in the daily-ness and busy-ness of life, help us to be aware of those around us who need You. Help us to learn from You to number our days and to apply our hearts unto wisdom that Your beauty may be upon us.*

"Forgive us for allowing prejudices and man-made barriers to keep us from sharing Your love with a desperately needy world."

Scripture Reading: John 4:1-42; Psalm 90:12-17; Matthew 9:36-38.

Introductory Insights: In John 4 we read of Jesus and the Samaritan woman at the well. At high noon, Jesus and His disciples arrived at Jacob's well, which was about one-half mile outside of Sychar. Because Jesus was very tired, He sat down and rested while His disciples went on into the city to get some provisions.

While Jesus was resting there, a woman from the city came out to the well to draw water. The exchange that took place between Jesus and the Samaritan woman is unusual for several reasons. First, the Jews and Samaritans were not on speaking terms. The Jews hated and looked down on the Samaritans (they were half-Jewish), and the feeling was reciprocated. Second, a man—especially a rabbi—was not to talk to a woman in public. Third, the woman was most likely not respected in the city since she was coming to draw water at a time when there was no one else there. She was a woman of ill repute. Fourth, Jesus asked a *personal* favor of her—that He might have a drink.

Digging into the Details:
1. *Read John 4:7-26.*

A. Considering the wide social and cultural gulf that separated Jesus from this woman, how did He get to her level?

B. Follow their dialogue. How did Jesus get from a "drink of water" to where the woman realized her personal need?

C. What did Jesus say that convinced her that He could be the Messiah?

2. *Read John 4:27-42.*

A. What was the disciples' reaction when they came back to the well and found Jesus and the Samaritan woman conversing?

B. From this passage, what convinces you that this woman sincerely believed in Jesus?

C. *Read verses 31-38.* List several important facts about evangelism that Jesus taught His disciples.

Further Reflections: After the woman shared her testimony with other Samaritans in her hometown, many came to listen to Jesus. The fact that many Samaritans believed fit in directly with Jesus' brief discourse with His disciples about the white harvest.

This "evangelism rally" hadn't been on the schedule; it simply happened. How often we miss opportunities to share the Gospel just because we're tired or intimidated, or worse, because we don't see the white harvest field. It is easy to become so caught up in the "stuff" of life that we lose all perspective and forget what is temporal and what is eternal.

Seeing the white harvest field does not mean we are "driven" or wrung out with the urgency of the message. Jesus ministered in the daily-ness of life: while eating and walking, while preaching in the synagogue, while attending weddings and funerals.

Jesus *went* about doing good, not *rushed* about doing good. But He didn't waste time, and used the most common, ordinary things to reach people. Above all, He was compassionate and met people at their point of need.

Points to Ponder:

❧ In pondering this thought of sharing the Gospel, how might you *personally* be more effective in your witness?

❧ What factors (if any) keep you from sharing with freedom and love?

❧ Can you think of any "unlikely" people with whom you have shared Christ? Where did you find your common ground that opened your conversation to deeper matters?

❧ Jesus talked to this woman without putting her down, yet through their conversation He pinpointed her need. How can we do this with those we talk to about Jesus?

The Key to Contentment

Today's Theme: Learning the discipline of contentment.

Moments in Prayer: *"Lord, help us to trust You and to choose an attitude of contentment in all circumstances. Amen."*

Scripture Reading: 1 Timothy 6:6-12; Hebrews 13:5-6; Philippians 4:11-13,19.

Digging into the Details:

1. *Learning our source of contentment.*

A. Reread 1 Timothy 6:6. Also read 1 Timothy 3:16 and 2 Peter 1:3-8. What does "godliness with contentment" mean?

B. List some temptations that face those who desire to be rich (1 Timothy 6:9-10).

C. Reread Hebrews 13:5-6. What difference does it make in our lives when our focus is on God as our source of contentment rather than man? (See also Psalm 118:5-9.)

2. *Learning the attitude of contentment.*

A. Considering all that Paul went through, how do you think he learned contentment (2 Corinthians 11:23-28)?

B. There are other enemies of contentment besides the desire for material gain. What can rob you of peace, and how can you combat it (Philippians 4:4-13)?

Further Reflections: Contentment speaks of security— knowing who you are, knowing your purpose in life and believing you are living out that purpose.

Sometimes we avoid settling for contentment because we fear apathy. We want to excel; we want the best—and that is good. The important thing is to check our focus. What are we striving to achieve? What is our purpose? How do we use things?

To be content or at peace, we must do the following:

1. *Feel gratitude toward God.* "Let the peace of Christ rule in your hearts, since as members of one body you were called to peace. And be thankful" (Colossians 3:15, NIV).

2. *Express trust toward God—by faith.* "And we know that all things work together for good to those who love God, to

those who are called according to *His* purpose" (Romans 8:28).

3. *Have an appropriate attitude toward things.* Paul the apostle learned how to live in need and in plenty (Philippians 4:12-13). Chuck Swindoll said, "If you love people, you will use *things*. If you love things, you will use *people*."

Often the things we chafe about in life have to do with our circumstances. There are many people in the Bible whose lives were completely changed when God intervened in the circumstances of their lives. You may want to study one or all of these individuals. Here are just a few:

> Joseph: Genesis 37–45
> Esther: Book of Esther
> Moses: Exodus 2–14
> Ruth: Book of Ruth
> David: 1 Samuel 16–2 Samuel 24

It is interesting to note that these individuals—even in their mistakes—tried to walk simply in obedience to God and did not seek the fame and fortune that were given to many of them. There are other individuals in the Bible—King Saul (1 Samuel 9–13) and Ananias and Sapphira (Acts 5)—who lost out with God because of their manipulation, deception and disobedience.

Points to Ponder: Perhaps the seed of discontentment is the subtle attitude that says, "God, I don't trust You for my life. I know what's better for me than You do, and I'm going to see that I get it."

How much better to pray: "Lord, give me a quiet, receptive and gentle spirit that is precious in Your sight. Help me to trust You with my very being—to walk in obedience before You and trust You with the result."